NECESSARY ROUGHNESS

NECESSARY ROUGHNESS

MIKE TROPE

with Steve Delsohn

CONTEMPORARY
BOOKS, INC.
CHICAGO • NEW YORK

Library of Congress Cataloging-in-Publication Data

Trope, Mike.
    Necessary roughness.

    1. Football—United States   2. Sports—United States—
Corrupt practices.   I. Delsohn, Steve.   Title.
GV951.T76   1987   796.332'0973   87-14083
ISBN 0-8092-4816-6

Published by Contemporary Books, Inc.
180 North Michigan Avenue, Chicago, Illinois 60601
Manufactured in the United States of America
Library of Congress Catalog Card Number: 87-14083
International Standard Book Number: 0-8092-4816-6

Published simultaneously in Canada by Beaverbooks, Ltd.
195 Allstate Parkway, Valleywood Business Park
Markham, Ontario L3R 4T8 Canada

For my grandmother, Jane Trope.
M.T.

For Mary Kay, whom I've always been looking for.
S.D.

CONTENTS

Thanks to Michael Lance Trope, for his kindness and generosity, and for making a difficult task enjoyable. Thanks to Shari Lesser, my editor, and Basil Kane, my agent, for their unique skills and diligence. Thanks, also, for their friendship. And thanks to all the talented people at Contemporary Books, who brought this book to life.

INTRODUCTION

Football is a violent game.

But the wars that erupt behind the scenes, beyond the public eye, are every bit as treacherous. Football, both professional and in college, has evolved into a multimillion-dollar industry. It's like any other Big Business: it gets dirty.

I became a sports agent in 1973. I was 21 years old, still a senior at the University of Southern California, still somewhat naïve. In my first eight years as an agent, I was the representative for six Heisman trophy winners. Over that same period, all before I turned 30 years old, I represented more Heisman winners, Heisman runners-up, number one picks, and first-round picks in the draft than any agent in the industry. I won't say I've seen it all, but I have seen a hell of a lot.

Last year I removed myself from the daily grind. Though I'm chairman of the board of a sports agency—Sports Corporation of America—I have no involvement in the day-to-day running of the business. In the wake of that decision,

5

I was asked to write a book about what I'd seen, what I'd experienced. It was something I'd long considered but for lack of time had put off. This time I agreed.

But I consented upon one condition: I wouldn't write a fairy tale. I'd portray the industry the way it really is. With all its blemishes.

That's what I've done. This book wasn't written in an ivory tower. The mentality isn't gee whiz, let's win one for the Gipper. Nor is this the typical agent's book: a self-congratulatory inventory of my client list or an abstract economics lesson.

This is a book about vengeance and ambition, humor and craziness. It's a book about wild, irresponsible players; conniving, eccentric owners; posturing, hypocritical college coaches; and ruthless, backstabbing agents. It's a book about a college kid who stumbled into a business, saw the way the game was played, and immediately understood something: there were times you had to play rough if you wanted to succeed.

In other words, it's a book about human beings.

NECESSARY ROUGHNESS

This is it, I thought; it's all over. Lawrence Taylor, All-Pro linebacker, one-on-one against Mike Trope. I've negotiated this great contract. Now I'm going to die for it.

1
L.T. & TRUMP: THE SECRET DEAL

There isn't a sports agent in the business who still has his soul. Hell, they sold them to the devil years ago.

I'll be the first to concede: among a wide majority of agents, ethics aren't a burning priority. However, the relationship between players and agents isn't as black and white as the press often makes it seem. There's another, muddier side to the business, one that people tend to ignore: sometimes it's the players who burn the agents.

In 1986, I exited the daily grind of agenting. And it was an incident like this one that weighed heavily in my decision.

This scenario involved a bit of everything: a superstar player, a high-ranking member of the NFL Players Association, an NFL team, a USFL team. It illustrates vividly the frustrations that can plague an agent. It also shows how deals get made and broken, and how fragile and temporary loyalties are. How personal gain—spell that *money*—takes precedence over all considerations.

In 1981, the New York Giants made Lawrence Taylor, then a linebacker from North Carolina, the number two choice in the NFL draft. As Lawrence's agent, I negotiated a six-year deal for him with the Giants. Including bonuses, it added up to roughly $1.5 million. Considering the state of the marketplace, we thought we were kicking ass.

Lawrence enjoyed an unprecedented rookie year. He was not only Defensive Rookie of the Year, but also Defensive Player of the Year, the first rookie ever to win that honor. Lawrence, coaches agreed, could dominate a game almost by himself. In 1982, though all of football was marred by the players' strike, Lawrence was again All-Pro.

In 1983, the marketplace changed drastically. The USFL was born, salaries in both leagues exploded. Subsequently, the contract Lawrence had signed as a rookie became outdated. Following his second year with the Giants, we attempted to renegotiate. The Giants agreed to add incentive clauses to Lawrence's contract immediately, but weren't prepared to tear it up and give him a new one. George Young, their general manager, said to come back at the end of Lawrence's third season. By then, he reasoned, half of Lawrence's original contract would have been completed, and the Giants would renegotiate in good faith. Young promised us a specific date: February 1, 1984. Lawrence and I agreed to that verbal commitment.

In November of 1983, with a few months remaining in Lawrence's third season, he phoned me in Los Angeles. The Giants were getting battered; his spirits were down. He was impatient about his future.

"Mike, I want you to come to New York and get this contract renegotiated," he said. "I want you to do it now. I need the peace of mind. I want to know I'm going to be taken care of."

I was surprised. "Lawrence, you know we've got an agreement with George Young to renew the deal in February," I said. "What difference does it make if we do it now or in February?"

Lawrence's voice rose. "The difference is that I'm your client and I want it done. And I want it done *now*."

I flew to New York and told Young: Lawrence wouldn't wait until after the season. Young wasn't pleased—we had given our word—but he agreed to work out a new deal that would take effect in 1984. Lawrence would get a $600,000 base salary in 1984, to be increased each year by $100,000, all the way up to $1.1 million by 1989. He'd also get a signing bonus up front for another $1 million. For six years, he'd earn roughly $7.3 million. The contract would easily make Lawrence the highest-paid defensive player in NFL history.

I left Young's office, elated, with the Giants' proposal on paper. That night, I went to see Lawrence with the news.

"You're going to love this, it's phenomenal," I said. "We tear up the existing three years on your contract, and we sign a new six-year deal."

Rather than exultant, Lawrence looked shocked. "What do you mean, a new *six*-year deal? I don't want anything longer than I've got now with the Giants. Three more years. That's it."

I was dumbfounded. "But Lawrence, you have to look at these numbers."

"I don't care what the numbers are. Three years, Mike. That's final."

That's when I showed him the Giants' new offer. As Lawrence read it, his mouth opened, and his jaw hung down. He put down the paper and put his face in both of his hands. He started rocking back and forth, gently. Like he was in pain.

By then I was *completely* confused. "Jesus, Lawrence, what's the matter?"

Lawrence took a deep breath. "I fucked up, man. I fucked up."

"You fucked up? What does that mean?"

"I fucked up," he repeated.

Then he dropped the bomb. "I already signed a contract

with the Generals," he said. "It starts in three years, after I'm through with the Giants. I can't believe this."

That made two of us. Lawrence had signed a futures contract with Donald Trump, owner of the New Jersey Generals of the USFL. Lawrence said the Generals were going to announce it in January at halftime of the Super Bowl to maximize the publicity.

It was a five-year option, to begin in 1988 when his contract with the Giants expired. Trump would give him a $1 million, interest-free loan immediately. Then, in 1988, Trump had the option of securing Lawrence's services. If he did, he would pay him $500,000 in 1988 and pop that up $100,000 a year for the next four years.

For the second time in 10 minutes, I was staggered. Compared to the deal I had just negotiated with the Giants, the Generals' numbers were ridiculous. Comparatively: In 1988, when Trump would be paying Lawrence $500,000, the Giants would be giving him $1 million. In 1989, when the Generals would be paying him $600,000, the Giants would be paying him $1.1 million. After 1989 with the Generals, Lawrence would still be tied up for three more years, and with a contract well below market value. After 1989 with the Giants, Lawrence would have completed his commitment. He would be free to make a brand-new deal.

Actually, it was worse than that. Because once the Giants discovered what Lawrence had done—that he'd signed with the USFL and for the next three seasons would be a lame duck—they'd immediately yank back their new offer. For his final three years in the NFL, Lawrence would be stuck with his now-outdated rookie contract. And there'd be more. Since Trump had made his deal with Lawrence *optional*, if Lawrence got injured, or his performance deteriorated, or Trump simply changed his mind, or the USFL folded, the Generals were not contractually bound to exercise their option. If that were to happen, all Lawrence would get from the Generals was the $1 million loan.

All told, I estimated that Lawrence, by accepting the

Generals' offer, would lose in the neighborhood of $2.4 million. And look like a fool, publicly, in the process.

Lawrence was right: he'd screwed up.

"Man," he said, "what are we going to do? You've got to get me out of this deal."

Lawrence had put me in a terribly awkward position—I had made a verbal agreement with George Young, then broken it at Lawrence's insistence—and I had still managed to get him a sweetheart of a new deal. While I was out doing that, Lawrence had gone and negotiated with another team, another league, without even a word to me.

I also knew that Lawrence Taylor doesn't just walk into Donald Trump's office and make a deal. There had to have been other parties involved. Someone had gotten to Lawrence.

I asked Lawrence to explain himself. His explanation as he told it to me, and later repeated it to my associate, Ivery Black, follows:

Lawrence originally got a phone call from a high-ranking officer of the NFL Players Association, a former player. He said he had a friend, a man who worked for Donald Trump, who wanted to speak with Lawrence about something confidential. Was it okay if he gave the man his phone number? Lawrence asked him if the man should first call his agent. The NFLPA officer said it wasn't necessary. This wasn't business, just a social call. Lawrence told him to give the man his number.

The man, Lawrence learned, worked as an aide to Trump and the Generals. He called Lawrence and invited him to come and meet Trump at Trump Tower for an informal chat. Lawrence met Trump at his headquarters. They didn't discuss any business. Lawrence was then ushered into a private room. Just he and the aide were there.

The aide told Lawrence that Trump wanted him to play for the Generals when his contract with the Giants expired in three years. Lawrence said they'd better call me. The aide said no—that would jeopardize the deal. He said Trump was a funny kind of a guy; he didn't like to deal with just anyone. There were certain types of people Trump respected; if Lawrence wanted to make the quickest, most satisfactory deal possible, he had to consult with someone Trump would respect. The aide knew just the man. He said there was a lawyer who represented a number of influential people, including congressmen and senators. Because of his powerful clients, he exerted influence over pieces of legislation—including real estate legislation—that could greatly aid or hinder a man in Trump's position. With that unique leverage, Trump's aide said, this attorney should be the only man to represent Lawrence in his negotiations with Trump.

The aide then called the NFLPA official, who had kick-started the chain of events in the first place, and he too attested to the attorney's efficiency. When Lawrence asked him if he should first see what the Giants were offering, he was told no by the NFLPA official, who said he had already spoken to someone in the Giants front office. According to him, the Giants weren't prepared to meet the Generals' numbers.

Lawrence and Trump's aide made an agreement: the attorney would come to New York and secretly negotiate a contract for Lawrence with the Generals. He soon came to New York and outlined a proposal for Lawrence. He asked him: if we can get this from Trump, do you want it? Lawrence hesitated; he asked again, shouldn't we go across the street and see what the Giants are offering? The attorney's no was emphatic. Not with a guy like Trump, he said. It could kill the deal.

The attorney soon returned to Lawrence and said the deal was consummated. Lawrence would begin playing for the Generals in 1988. Lawrence signed the contract, with the agreement that neither side would announce the signing until halftime of the Super Bowl.

When Lawrence finished, I was speechless. It was quite a scheme, but I couldn't help thinking that someone other than Trump had devised it. All Trump knew, I believed, was that he wanted Lawrence Taylor. I had no doubt that it was Trump's aide, acting on his own volition, who had put together the details.

In any case, Trump, who loved publicity almost as much as he loved rubbing salt in the NFL's wounds, would accomplish both at once, embarrassing the rival league during its brightest moment. Lawrence could have me— without any knowledge of his deal with the Generals—ask for a richer deal from the Giants. Not until halftime of the Super Bowl, when it was too late, would the Giants learn they'd been suckered.

It almost worked. Had Lawrence not told me about his deal with the Generals, it very well might have. As it was, I had indeed gone to the Giants and asked them for Lawrence's raise. But now Lawrence realized that he, too, had been used.

After he told me the entire story, I went to see Trump's aide. I put both teams' numbers on the table, showing him that Lawrence would lose over $2 million if his contract with the Generals held. I said they had screwed Lawrence, and now he wanted out.

He said no, that Taylor was the Generals' property, and that was that. He was adamant. I demanded to deal directly with Trump.

Trump Tower, a glass and bronze skyscraper, sits on Manhattan's Fifth Avenue among Bloomingdale's and Tiffany's. Everything about it reeks of wealth. Outside Trump's personal office, as I waited for our meeting, I was shown a slick, five-minute slide show about Trump Tower. Sinatra sang "New York, New York" in the background. Just as the lights went back on, I was told that Mr. Trump was ready to see me. Nice touch; I could see how Lawrence might have been overwhelmed.

Despite the trappings of his building, Trump's own office, though nicely done, was not extravagant. Neither was Trump's manner: he seemed sharp and aggressive, but congenial and willing to listen. A man you couldn't pull much over on, but one you could reason with.

I told Trump the same thing I had told his aide: Lawrence's contract with the Generals would cost him at least $2 million down the road. I showed him the Giants' numbers. I said it was a terrible deal for Lawrence.

"I want to tell you something else," I said. "I realize you have Taylor locked into this contract. But you've just lent $1 million to a player who you don't even know will play for you. It's four years away. Taylor could get injured or whatever. It's a bad deal for Taylor, and it's a bad deal for you. You've been ill advised by your aide."

Trump considered that for a moment. Then he smiled. "Do you think you can work something out with the Giants, so I can still make a profit on the deal?" he asked. He wanted me to see if the Giants would pay him for releasing Lawrence from his contract. I told Trump I would see what I could do.

I respect George Young; I think he's one of the more able GMs in the league. Feeling awkward and depressed that things had come to this, I met with him for lunch. He still knew nothing of what had transpired. To the contrary, he believed the subject of our meeting was Lawrence's new contract with the Giants. When I told Young that his best player had already signed a contract—not only with the rival league, but with Donald Trump—Young looked physically ill. I didn't feel too well either.

I asked Young: before the press gets ahold of this, can I go back and forth, between the two teams, and try to work something out to get Lawrence back to the Giants? Young told me to see what I could do. But his expression was doubtful.

Over the next two weeks, I conducted some of the toughest, most intricate negotiations of my career. First there were the Giants to contend with. Though they were reacting like gentlemen considering the situation, I had to go to great lengths to convince them I wasn't in collusion with Trump and that I was indeed dealing in good faith.

Trump was also presenting problems. After five or six meetings, he still wanted more from the Giants than they were willing to give. Finally I laid it on the line: "Look, this is all you're going to get out of this thing. There's an old saying: pigs get fat, hogs get slaughtered. If Lawrence were to get severely injured, there's a chance you could wind up with nothing."

Trump relented; he said to go ahead and make the deal. I made it. Lawrence Taylor went back to the Giants.

Here's how it worked: Lawrence paid back Trump the $1 million loan, with some interest. Trump also got a $750,000 buy-out in return for releasing Lawrence from his contract. Although Trump technically received the buy-out from Lawrence, in reality part of it came from the pockets of the Giants, who sweetened their deal with Lawrence to make the buy-out more acceptable to him. Lawrence, meanwhile, got the original offer from the Giants, plus the sweeteners, making him the highest-paid defensive player in NFL history.

After the buy-out became public, there was tremendous publicity. Some observers felt Trump got what he had wanted in the first place: publicity and profit. But I don't think it was that simple. As for the profit, I doubt a man of Trump's wealth was doing cartwheels over $750,000. There's no question he welcomed the ink, but not just for its own sake. Trump, I believe, was considering the larger picture. I think his goal, all along, was to use the USFL to drive NFL salaries so high that the older league would come begging on its hands and knees for a merger. Stealing Lawrence would have been one more piece, a glamorous one, of the puzzle.

Trump told me as much. He said he knew signing a Lawrence Taylor or a Herschel Walker would cost him several million dollars, but it would cost the NFL many, many more millions, because of the ripple effect on salaries. Trump seemed to take great delight in the fact that he, single-handedly, could cause NFL owners to spend millions of dollars they otherwise never would have.

As for releasing Lawrence from his contract, I believe Trump also had a more humanitarian motive. He simply didn't want to hurt Lawrence Taylor.

I think Trump looked at the numbers, saw how much money Lawrence would be losing, and felt compassion for him. Yes, he would have loved to show up the NFL, but not at the expense of stealing money from Lawrence Taylor. Trump knew Lawrence could never be happy leaving $2 million on the table. So he let him go.

In our two weeks of negotiations, I gained tremendous respect for Trump. You can't deny the man's ego, but he did something for Lawrence that most management never would have.

Trump has something else: balls. It took balls to give Lawrence $1 million on a contract that didn't begin for another four years. It was Trump's money, his risk of embarrassment if Lawrence got hurt. But he was willing to take it, to make a statement to the other league. It's the only time I've ever seen anything like it in sports.

I'd love to tell you the saga of Lawrence Taylor ended there. Except that it didn't.

It was mid-January 1984 before we got the whole thing straightened out. With the final contract from the Giants, my associate Ivery Black and I went over to Lawrence's house. After Lawrence signed the contracts, he asked, "By the way, is this contract guaranteed?"

"No," I said. "Other than the front money, if the Giants want to cut you, they do have the right to cut you."

Lawrence bolted out of his seat. "What? What kind of shit is this? You got me a contract that wasn't guaranteed?"

The fact is, guaranteed NFL contracts are rare. For the most part it just isn't done; careers are too tenuous. Lawrence knew that. Besides, I told Lawrence, the contract he had with the Generals—which tied him up for the next nine years of his career for much less money—hadn't been guaranteed either.

Lawrence started cursing me, violently. Then he stormed out the door without a word.

I looked at Mrs. Taylor, then at Ivery. "This is incredible!" I said. "We just busted our ass to get him out of a terrible deal, and into a great one, and he isn't happy. I feel like I'm in the 'Twilight Zone.'"

A moment later, Lawrence reappeared at the door. His eyes were all red; he looked like he'd been crying. He didn't say anything. He started stalking directly toward me.

My breath went short. This is it, I thought; it's all over. Lawrence Taylor, All-Pro linebacker, one-on-one against Mike Trope. I've negotiated this great contract. Now I'm going to die for it.

But when Lawrence got to me, his face softened. He embraced me in a bear hug and lifted me off the ground, apologizing profusely and saying he was ashamed. He said it was a great goddamn contract; having no guarantee would be the best thing for his career. He'd have to work that much harder to remain at the top of his game.

The next morning I was back in Los Angeles. But I still felt uneasy about the whole experience. Mostly it was the bizarre incident the night before at his home. Lawrence's emotions had swung so wildly, from hatred to gratitude, that my own emotions responded in kind, from physical dread to nervous relief. Normally, when a deal was done I could put it aside. This time I still felt unsettled.

Something else was still irritating me: the impetus for the entire incident. I'd seen my share of strange bedfellows, but the teaming of management, an attorney, and a leading figure in the NFL Players Association was an unholy alliance if ever there was one.

The aide's motives were easily discernible: he was trying to get Lawrence for the Generals at the lowest possible price. The attorney's were equally clear: he wanted to represent Lawrence (although he either sold him out or didn't know what the hell he was doing, because he cut him a lousy deal).

It was the NFLPA official's intentions that didn't fit. Why would he, a leading official of the NFLPA, try to steer a player to a rival league? Why would an official of the

NFLPA, a body that intercedes in contract disputes between players and management, encourage a star like Lawrence to sign for such low terms? Why would an official of the NFLPA, when asked by Lawrence if he should first see what the Giants were offering, tell Lawrence no?

Something, it seemed obvious at the time, was rotten. Over the past few years, my suspicions have only been reinforced. First, shortly after the Taylor incident, the official quit the NFLPA. Personally, I believe it was a cover-up, that he was pushed out by the union for his tremendous liability in the Taylor affair. The entire incident, I believe, was conveniently swept beneath the rug.

Then, in January of 1986, he went to work at a sports agency. One of his partners was the attorney.

Still naked, he jumped back on the bed and began performing an animated rendition of a woman in rapture, complete with panting and rolling eyes. At the final buzzer, so to speak, he was banging his head off the headboard, screaming his own name in a falsetto voice like a woman in ecstasy. He stopped just short of smoking a cigarette.

2
THE WILD, *WILD* WORLD OF SPORTS

In the course of my career, I've negotiated contracts that add up to somewhere in the neighborhood of $200 million. It's a pretty nice neighborhood. Big-time agent, big-time finance. Sounds glamorous.

In a sense perhaps it is. But as you'll be able to tell by the stories I'm about to relate, I've also been something else at times: an extremely high-priced babysitter.

If you're an agent, whether it's in Hollywood or the NFL, you'd better be prepared to hold some hands. I didn't particularly care for the responsibility, definitely didn't anticipate it before I entered the business, but quickly accepted it as part of the terrain—part of what I was getting paid, and paid well, for.

I'm not making a blanket statement. Many athletes I encountered were mature, levelheaded, considerate. They were adults. They didn't need anyone, particularly some agent, to remind them.

I've also seen athletes act like 12-year-olds. Some were just fools, just like there are agents, plumbers, and doctors who are fools. I don't want to spend a lot of time analyzing why some athletes do crazy things; I'm not a psychologist. But I do believe when signing up professional athletes, there's a larger context which goes largely ignored: it's a lifestyle that could change just about anybody.

It's the adulation. People do things for athletes they don't do for others. When an athlete needs some credit, even if his finances are in a shambles, he walks into a bank and gets it. Best table at a crowded restaurant? No problem. You can't make that appearance you promised you would? It's okay, we understand, you're busy. To you and me, people say no, make us suffer the consequences of our behavior. Not athletes. Until they retire, "no" isn't a word they hear much.

The outcome? Values are modified, sometimes misplaced entirely. Even good guys, humble guys, are vulnerable to change. Not always. But I've seen it happen a lot.

Add this to the mix: the fear of losing everything with one injury, the sleaze coming at them from every direction, the inflated expectations. It can spin almost any man's head around; it just isn't a "normal" way to live. And when you evaluate the total package of a player's personality, particularly someone who's recently out of college, I think you have to factor in all those considerations.

I always did. It kept me sane.

A millionaire NFL owner is not going to bust his ass to go meet a prospective backup punter. The star quarterback he's about to give the vault to, that's another story.

Normally, the preliminary meeting between owner and star is fairly predictable: you're great, the team's great, the city's great, let's pound lunch and get the hell out of here.

That's how it usually happens.

But not always.

I once represented a player with considerable talent, when his NFL contract was terminated by mutual agreement between him and the club. Two other teams courted him immediately. One of those teams flew him and me to their

city, where they put us up in the presidential suite of a
beautiful hotel. We each had private rooms, with a common
adjoining door. The owner and his executives would be up
to see us in an hour.

My client said he would be resting in his room; I should
knock on the door when it was time for our meeting. Before
he left I warned him: "Stay on your good behavior. I want
to get as much money out of these people as we possibly
can."

He shrugged and told me not to worry. I worried.

This was more than typical precaution. I had been told
that the owner was a conservative, sophisticated man. My
client, on the other hand, was an unadulterated screwup. I
had an inkling they might clash, and I didn't want to
jeopardize the deal.

There was a knock on my door an hour later. It was our
hosts, in full force: the owner, general manager, and
director of public relations. We small-talked, then I asked
them if they were ready to meet my client. I knocked on the
door and he said to come on in.

When we entered, he was lying on his bed. No big deal;
he'd probably been napping. But there was something else,
something just a tiny bit unusual.

He was totally naked.

His legs were stretched out across the length of the bed.
He had a pillow perched behind his head, his left hand
wedged beneath the pillow. His right hand was scratching
his balls.

Frankly, I would have liked to strangle the guy, but they
have laws against that type of thing. With no alternative, I
introduced him.

"Mr. Owner," I said, "I'd like you to meet my client."

My esteemed client stood up, removed his right hand
from his balls, and offered it to the owner to shake. The
owner just stood there, paralyzed. The player kept his hand
there, grinning.

Finally, like a man accepting a glass of poison, the owner

took the player's hand. Their cultures clashed, and at first they missed connections. The owner went Traditional; the player went for the Soul Shake. On the next attempt they compromised, sort of a combo shake.

The owner asked him how he liked their fair city.

"Well," he said, "that depends on the double P."

"Uh, I'm afraid I don't understand," said the owner, not at all sure that he wanted to. "What, uh, what is the Double P?"

"That's the pussy and the paper," said the player. "Because if the Double P is all right, then I'll like this place just fine."

What he meant, in English, was the women and the money. The owner apparently understood the part about the women. "Well, uh," said the owner, "I, uh, could give you a couple of phone numbers if you like."

"Yeah, yeah, right," said the player, not really listening. "Hey, Mr. Owner, let me ask you a personal question."

The owner looked like he might cry.

"Do you likes to go down on your women?" the player asked.

"What?"

"You know, do you likes to eats that pussy?"

The owner winced. "Well, I, uh, ahem . . ."

" 'Cause man," the player cut him off, "I had this bitch back home before I got out here . . ."

Still naked, he jumped back on the bed and began performing an animated rendition of a woman in rapture, apparently the woman upon whom he had performed oral sex the evening before, complete with panting and rolling eyes. At the final buzzer, so to speak, he was banging his head off the headboard, screaming his own name in a falsetto voice like a woman in ecstasy. He stopped just short of smoking a cigarette.

I stole a glance at the owner and his associates. They didn't look so good.

I mumbled something to my client and shuffled with the

team representatives back to my room. I didn't know what to say; "He's quite a guy" didn't seem appropriate. I just said I'd speak with them in the morning.

I sat on my bed, still in shock. Not only was it one of the most bizarre moments of my life, but I'd flown all the way there for nothing. Sign him? He'd be lucky if they didn't have him arrested. The deal was history. End of story.

Wrong. That night I got a call from the owner's daughter. Would we like to join her for dinner? Somewhat shocked, I told her we would.

Dinner went smoothly, as if the afternoon's nightmare had never happened. In fact, my client and the owner's daughter hit it off quite well—they ended up spending the night together.

A few days later, he signed a contract with her father.

Shoot first, ask questions later.

It's a phrase I often used to describe the habits of certain clients. They would blunder into some predicament, then come running back to me to help dig them out.

I was once in a fancy Los Angeles restaurant, having dinner with a client and his attorney. The previous fall, my client had been one of the most celebrated players in college football. Now it was July, a few days before his first NFL training camp.

The player's attorney, unschooled in negotiating sports contracts, had screened several other agents before deciding on me. As a result, I didn't meet the player until much later in the agent/client process than I normally would. I hardly knew him, but he seemed clean-cut. His appearance was conservative, and he was handsome and very articulate. If there was still such a thing as the All-American boy, he qualified.

I was shocked, then, in the middle of dinner, when the attorney told his player to stay off drugs for the next few days.

The player's new team, the attorney warned, would be

issuing physical examinations. The player swore he would abstain. It wasn't even an issue, he said. Those problems were behind him.

When the player excused himself to use the rest room, I questioned the attorney. He said the player had once had a problem with cocaine but was now "on the straight and narrow." He just didn't want any slipups.

A few days later the player left for camp. The day he arrived he called me at my home. He sounded scared, panicked.

"Look, man, I've got a problem," he said. "The team is taking physicals, and they're taking urine samples," he said.

"So what's the problem?" I asked.

He was silent for a long moment. "Well, I went to a party last night and snorted some coke. It'll show up in my sample. Man, what do I do?"

I didn't know what the hell to tell him. I was irritated that I'd even been put in that position; I felt it exceeded my responsibilities as an agent. It was also the first time in my career I'd been confronted with this particular situation. What was I supposed to do, call up the team and tell them my client snorted cocaine, he can't go through with the physical?

If I'd had more time to think, I'm not sure what I would have told him. As it was, I told him to leave. Just pack his stuff, get on a plane, and go home. So he did.

All hell broke loose that day. The press wanted to know why such a highly acclaimed rookie would bolt from his first pro camp. I was at a loss for words. What finally came out was purposely vague: I said there were people in the team's front office who hadn't treated my client with dignity, with the proper respect that a first-round pick deserved. So I had him leave. The reporters accepted the explanation (this was before the word *drugs* popped into people's minds anytime an athlete did something irrational).

I felt horrible. I pride myself on my honesty; lying so

blatantly left an ugly aftertaste. Worse, I had always enjoyed a warm relationship with the team's general manager; our dealings had been civilized and mutually respectful. But now, like everyone else, he was bewildered. He called me for an explanation.

I told him that something must have happened at camp, because my client had told me he was unhappy there. And I had told him to go home. I apologized; maybe I'd reacted too quickly, I said. He was irate, disappointed in me. I couldn't blame him.

The heat came down, hard, directly on me. The press moved in for the kill. For the next three days, I had to read about what a son of a bitch Mike Trope was, dealing in poor faith, yanking a rookie from his first pro camp. It was a tidy scenario: the innocent athlete, this model citizen, getting sold down a misguided path by his villainous agent.

I fumed, but silently. It was all part of the game.

Take an athlete and give him a lot of money. Put his name in the morning paper, his face on the evening news. He's got what a lot of people lust for: wealth and fame.

He's also a target.

It's the downside of celebrity. Every hustler, con man, and parasite wants a piece of you. They hang out in hotel bars and outside locker rooms, with expensive German cars and Italian suits. They've all got a surefire deal, a corner-cutting path to the top.

Some athletes are intelligent enough and sufficiently wary to fend off the predators. Others aren't. I once had a client who very nearly got hustled for $100,000. It happened in the seventies, back when $100,000, even to a pro athlete, was an awful lot of money.

He had recently signed a contract with an NFL team, and as the team convened for training camp several weeks later, I got a call from the GM. Great, I thought, he wants to tell me how pleased he is with my client.

"What the hell are you trying to do?" the GM yelled.
"Get me fired down here?"

"Slow down, slow down," I said, startled. "Tell me what
happened."

"I'll tell you what happened. Your guy showed up at
training camp 25 pounds overweight. He looks like a
goddamn bowling ball."

I told the GM this was the first I'd heard of it and
promised I would call the player immediately. I hung up
the phone and dialed my client.

He didn't need football, he said. Hell, yeah, his career
was young, but maybe it was time for him to move on to
bigger things. He could make so much more money outside
of football. Then, as if it were an afterthought, he said I'd
be receiving a phone call from a guy he knew (I'm going to
call him Smith).

He said Smith, a prominent Hollywood producer and
friend of the family, had lent his mother $100,000. Now
Smith wanted his money back. Sure, his mother had acted
impulsively, but as her son he was obligated to help her.
Everything was cool—he was going to pay Smith $60,000,
as well as give him one of his $40,000 cars. His mom, then,
would be off the hook.

To put it mildly, I was skeptical. "Your mother borrowed
$100,000 from this guy?" I asked. "What the hell for?"

"It's personal," he said. "And Mike, don't fuck this thing
up, because this guy's a hotshot producer. And if he gets
back his money quick enough, he's going to put me in a
major motion picture."

I hadn't bought the part about his mom borrowing a
hundred grand in the first place. When he started talking
about the movies, I knew it was bullshit. My client, I was
sure, had fabricated the story; he figured it was the only way
I'd ever let him give this guy $100,000. His real intentions,
I didn't know yet.

I wanted to see where this was leading. I played dumb; I

told him I would talk to Smith and get back to him.

Smith called that afternoon. His voice was deep, melodramatic; it reminded me of James Earl Jones.

"Well, there's probably a slight discrepancy in what you've been told," Smith said. "In reality, the boy's mother owes me more than $100,000."

"Is that right?" I asked. "How much more?"

"That's not important, Mr. Trope. Because I've decided to call it even if the lad pays back the $100,000. I feel badly for this young lad and his family, and I want to help them out in any way I can. What I've decided to do for him is make him one of the stars of my upcoming movie. It's called *The Opium Jungle.* Perhaps you've heard about it."

I hadn't.

"Well, Mr. Trope, it's a tremendous opportunity for the boy. He'll be playing across from a very famous actor. I'm giving James Caan $3 million to play the lead."

When I didn't respond, Smith continued. "As for your client, once his family and I are even, I'll pay him another $100,000 in return for performing in my film. He'll be on his way toward a long career as an actor."

Right, and I'm Vanna White. I told Smith I would get back to him.

I called my client's mother. She said she had never borrowed a dime from anyone, let alone $100,000, which confirmed my doubts about my client's story. I was sure Smith did actually offer him a role in a movie if he'd put up $100,000 in collateral. But as I'd suspected, he or Smith, or both, had made up the part about the loan. After doing my own investigation, I discovered the rest of the deal. Smith had offered him a movie role, but only if he first put up $100,000. Supposedly, Smith had all this money coming in from Singapore to finance the movie. But since Smith needed capital in the interim, and since my budding movie star wanted to be in the movie, they made a deal: if my client would put up $100,000, Smith would repay him as soon as the money arrived from Singapore; he'd also pay him another $100,000 for appearing in the film.

This is why football players need agents.

Next I wanted to check out this blockbuster movie. I knew James Caan spent a lot of time at Hugh Hefner's mansion, so I made a call to a woman I was dating, a former Playboy bunny; I asked her for the number there. Eventually, I got ahold of Caan and introduced myself. I told him one of my clients was being offered a part in a film called *The Opium Jungle*. I told him that Smith had said he would be the star.

Caan made a snorting sound. "Look, I'm not in the movie, and I've never heard of the movie," he said. "But this isn't the first time this Smith guy has used my name. As far as I know, there is no movie and he isn't even a producer. He's just another bullshit artist."

I told Caan the whole story. He was surprised that the player had fallen for such an asinine ruse. And he agreed to help straighten things out.

I called my client, told him I had James Caan on the other line. The player was ecstatic. I put Caan on the line.

"Mr. Caan, I'm such a great fan of yours," my client gushed. "I can't believe we're going to star together in a movie."

"Look, kid, I'm not in any movie called *The Opium Jungle*," Caan said. "I'm sorry. The movie doesn't exist."

My client was stunned. "What do you mean you're not in the movie?" he said. "I know you are. I saw some papers with your name on them."

"Hey," said Caan, a little irritated, "this is James Caan you're *talking* to. And I'm telling you I'm *not* in that movie. Not for $3 million, not for three bucks. There is no movie. You're getting snowed."

The player started in again about the papers bearing Caan's name. Caan cut him off sharply.

"Look, nobody just walks into the movie industry, including you," Caan said. "There's no shortcuts; it doesn't work that way. You're a football player, not an actor. If you were smart, you'd get your mind and your body back into playing football."

Caan hung up. I stayed on the line with my client, and I told him I had spoken to his mother, that I knew he had lied to me. His voice cracked; he sounded on the verge of tears. He told me Smith had promised him a huge career in the movies. I'd guessed right: he knew I'd never say yes to the 100 grand without the story about his mom.

He apologized for lying to me. "But what should I do now?" he said. "I already gave this guy my car. And ten thousand bucks."

Great.

From everything I'd heard, Smith didn't sound like an amateur. I had a criminal search done on him. Dating all the way back to 1951, he'd been arrested for a series of offenses: forgery, stock schemes and pandering, among others.

I called Smith and told him what I knew. "It's over, pal," I said. "I looked up your record. You're a fraud. You're trying to steal $100,000 from my client."

I expected one of two things: Smith would either slam down the phone or threaten me, like any other thug. What I didn't expect was for Smith to sound hurt. Deeply, terribly hurt.

"Oh no," he moaned, "it's happening to me again. It's happening to me again. Why can't this stop happening to me?"

I asked him what he was talking about.

"So help me, Mike, there are *two* people out there with my name. And it's the *other* one who has the criminal record. No matter where I go, this problem plagues me. Just because this man was born with the same name as I, this terrible cloud surrounds me. Tell me, Mike, why can't this stop happening to me?"

Jesus, this guy didn't quit. "I don't care who the hell you are," I said. "You're not getting any more money. I spoke to

James Caan. He told me you're full of shit and that there is no movie. We'll be by your house for the car. The $10,000 you've already got, I'm sure you've already spent. We'll work that out later."

My client was tremendously relieved. He never salvaged his $10,000—he didn't want to file charges, probably to avoid the embarrassing press—but at least he got back his $40,000 car. I think he also learned his lesson. He got back in shape and back to reality.

There was one day in my office when reality seemed to be suspended. It was one of the strangest, most disturbing incidents in my career.

Around noon, my client, a gigantic young lineman, walked into my office unannounced. He didn't say hello. He just walked straight to my big glass window and stood there, staring out at the Los Angeles skyline.

Maybe he was just apprehensive. Several weeks from now would be one of the turning points in his life: the NFL draft. But when he looked at me, I could see that his problem was more than nerves. His eyes were red and frightened. He was a bright, thoughtful kid; normally he'd flop into my easy chair, and we'd have these long, esoteric discussions. Now he couldn't stand still. He paced across the room, stopped, and peered again out my window.

"I came in to say good-bye," he said. "I'm going now."

"You're *going* now?" I said. "What the hell does that mean? Where are you going?"

"I'm jumping out this motherfucking window," he said. "Right now. I came in to say good-bye."

He was obviously distressed, but of course he was exaggerating; I knew there was no real danger.

Or was there? When he kept gazing out the window, I got nervous. I walked over to him, slowly, and guided him to his usual chair. He sat down. Then he put his face in his hands and cried.

He told me that his wife wanted a divorce, that he was a

failure, that there really was no reason to continue his life. He said it was "over," and he was just coming in to say good-bye to me. Mingled with his tears, the words spilled out so fast I could hardly understand him. I was beginning to wonder if he had been using drugs.

For the next three-and-a-half hours I barely stopped talking. He would start crying; he would threaten to jump; I would tell him how much he had going for him, how bright his future was. This went on all afternoon. Finally I called a student I knew he was close to. Would she come pick up her friend? He needed serious help.

She drove to my office, picked him up, and drove him directly to the psychiatric ward of a Los Angeles hospital.

Several weeks later, in the last 10 days before the draft, I began receiving the traditional calls from various GMs around the league who were interested in my client. I told them he was indisposed; he'd gotten so nervous about the draft, he'd gone away on a fishing trip. He hadn't, of course. He was still recovering in the psychiatric ward.

It turned out he'd taken a hallucinogenic drug, a brutally powerful tranquilizer normally administered to animals. They kept him in the hospital until two days before the draft. On the day of the draft, my client became a first-round pick. He went on to have a long, successful pro career. As far as I know, he never went back to drugs.

That was a case of a player who trusted me completely. Unfortunately, there are always those players who don't trust anyone. Including their agents.

Once, at a player's request, I took him to the bank so he could open a checking account. I had nothing to do with the account—no power of attorney, nothing. I just took him to the bank. He deposited $50,000.

Six weeks later he called me, and in a very accusatory tone demanded that I come to his home and go over his bank statement. He said some of his money was missing, implying that I had something to do with it.

I forced myself not to lose my temper; it wasn't worth the aggravation. I went to his house and looked at his statement. Of the original $50,000, only $16,000 was left. I went through all his checks and added them up. Over a six-week period, he had written $34,000 worth of checks for items like televisions, stereos, and a truck.

"Take a look here," I said. "When you add up all your checks, then you add that total to your current balance, it equals $50,000."

His wife, who'd been sitting in a chair, minding her own business, suddenly jumped up.

"Goddamn fool," she yelled.

No one had stolen his money. He had spent it.

Sometimes, in their demands, the guys get a little carried away. I had a client call me once complaining that his air conditioner had broken. He wanted me to drive across Los Angeles to his home and fix it.

But that was nothing compared to the saga of the shaking bed.

I was 22 years old, working out of town to negotiate a contract. The deal went well, and the player insisted on taking me out to show his appreciation. Though it was already close to midnight, he talked me into it.

We went to a disco. Apparently he was a regular; minutes after we arrived, he was completely surrounded by women. That was the last I saw of him for about an hour.

I sat alone at our table, bored, tired, nursing a beer, eager to leave. My client resurfaced at closing time, with an Amazon blonde about six feet tall with breasts the size of Cleveland. He seemed sober. She seemed smashed, uttering words in no particular sequence.

The three of us drove back to my client's house, where I was spending the night as a guest. I was in his guest bedroom, reading, when I heard a knock on my door. It was my client, smiling broadly. He had a quarter in his hand.

"Let's go, let's flip," he said.

"Flip?" I asked.

"Flip the coin," he said, "to see who goes to bed with her first."

I laughed nervously and hoped he was joking. He wasn't.

"No, no, no," I said. "I don't want to go to bed with her. She doesn't want to go to bed with me. Let me go to sleep. You picked her up; she's with you."

"Man," he said, "she's so bombed, and it's so dark in my room, she won't know *who* she's with. Now flip."

I was getting irritated. I told him to go ahead and flip. If I lost, they could do as they pleased. If I "won," I'd just renege; I'd still tell him he was crazy and go to sleep.

I called heads. It was heads.

I told him, again, I had no desire to sleep with his friend. He got incredibly upset and offended. He said he couldn't believe I didn't appreciate his gesture.

He said to get in the room or he would fire me.

This presented an intriguing dilemma, one I'd never seen in my agent's handbook. I didn't have a lot of clients at that point, he was a good one, and I didn't particularly want to lose him over something as ridiculous as this. I also didn't want to go to bed with this woman.

I had an idea. I said okay, okay, smiled at him resignedly, and walked into his room.

He was right: it was pitch black in there. No wonder; everything *was* black—the drapes, the walls, the bedspreads. The woman, naked, was lying on his bed. She was asleep. Or seriously passed out. I went to the foot of the bed, and started shoving it back and forth, banging the headboard up against the wall. I did this for four or five minutes. I kept expecting her to jump up and ask me what the hell I thought I was doing, but, fortunately, she never stirred.

I finally stopped slamming the bed, waited a minute or two, and walked out of the bedroom. He was standing in the hallway, waiting, grinning like a fool. He demanded I give him slaps, then he let me go to bed.

I guess the woman left before I woke up. In the morning, the player and I went out to breakfast and ran into some of his friends, who joined us. Then he started bragging about the evening before.

"You should have heard it," he said with delight. "He almost knocked the wall over."

I didn't feel like a total idiot. Just about 95 percent.

Not shocking, but definitely true: in the course of my career, that was not the only case of women succumbing to the charms of my clients. To please the athlete of their choice, I've seen women go to extraordinary lengths.

I was once invited to a party with a client. He had a date, and I didn't. He offered to fix me up with a woman he'd met. At the time I was single, no girlfriend. Why not?

When I picked her up, she wasn't ready. She invited me in while she finished getting dressed. She was in her mid-20s, very attractive. Not too friendly, though, like it was an effort just to say hello.

I've had better dates. Once we got to the party, she didn't give me the time of night. She couldn't have if she'd wanted to; she was too busy crawling all over the athletes.

Several weeks later, back in Los Angeles, I was chatting with a player I knew; he said he was going out of town, to the same city where I'd had my blind date. Did I know any women there?, he asked. I thought about the date, the party. I had a feeling, just a hunch, she had a thing for athletes. I dug up her phone number and gave it to him.

Later that week the player called me from the road. He sounded like he'd just hit the lottery.

"Mike Trope, goddamn, you are the greatest," he screamed into the phone. "Anything you want, it's yours. Goddamn, you're the greatest."

"I guess the date went well," I said.

"Are you serious? This woman is in goddamn love with me. She came to my hotel, and now I can't get her to leave. She's insatiable. Trope, I owe you."

As things turned out, she wasn't your ordinary lust-ridden groupie. She was equally generous with her check-book. Shirts, sweaters, hats, shoes—he didn't ask for a thing—she just went out and bought them for him. By the time the weekend ended, he was dressing like the guys in *GQ.*

A few weeks later, I found a strange letter in my mailbox. It was for the player, but sent to my address. Then I recognized the return address. It was from the nympho shopper.

I called the player and told him she had sent him a letter. Why, I asked him, had she sent it to me?

"Because I told her to," he replied.

"Why'd you do that?"

"Where's she supposed to send it, my place? My girlfriend would kill me."

"I don't believe this," I said. "What do you want me to do with it?"

"Read it to me."

"What?"

"Read it to me now, over the phone. Come on, what the hell."

I read him the letter. Imagine the dirtiest, most suggestive thing you've ever read. Now multiply that by 10.

Also enclosed was a picture. Apparently she had one of those cameras where you can set the timer, run and get in place, and take a picture of yourself. Or else she had a friend take the picture. In any case, she was standing naked in the bathtub, shaving one of her armpits. All she wore was this big, dumb smile.

With the women, the glamor, the fame, do all athletes live in their own not-so-real world? Not all of them, but just enough to keep the average agent slightly off balance. Not to mention his wife.

It was early 1980, 11 o'clock at night. When I got home, my wife Patty was sitting up in bed. She was laughing.

"What are you in such a good mood about?" I said.

Patty started to say something, stopped, and started giggling again.

"Come on," I said. "what's so funny?"

Patty said she'd just gotten off the phone with Russell Erxleben. Russell was a punter with the New Orleans Saints, out of the University of Texas; I had represented him in his rookie year. (The Saints, by the way, gave Russell a signing bonus of $320,000, which was then the largest signing bonus in history for a punter or kicker.)

Patty was still laughing as she related what Russell had said to her. She said he'd called in an outrage, and their conversation went like this:

"Patty, this is Russell Erxleben. Where's Mike?"

"He's out, but I'm sure he'll be home in a little while."

"Well, you make sure you have that boy call me right quick the minute he comes home."

"Sure, Russell. Is there something wrong?"

"Well, since you're part of the family I guess I can tell you. Yes, I think you should know. Are you standing up or sitting down?"

"I'm sitting down. Russell, what is it?"

"Now just hear me out. Don't say a thing until I'm finished talking. Last weekend, when your husband told you he was off on some business trip to New York, he wasn't on no business trip to New York. He was in New York all right, but he wasn't doing business. He was sleeping with my ex-wife, Ava, in a hotel room. And three weeks before that, when he told you he was down in Miami doing business? He was in New York again, sleeping with my ex-wife, Ava."

"You're sure of this, Russell?"

"Patty, they're having an affair; they're making fools out of you and me. They've been going at it hot and heavy for a month and a half. Mike ain't going on no business trips. He's sleeping with Ava."

Russell and Ava, high school sweethearts, had been married about the time that Russell became a pro. The marriage hadn't worked; within a year they were divorced. Now, though Russell had already remarried, he still didn't want his ex-wife to see other men. That was their business. But I hadn't even *seen* Ava since the day Russell had signed his contract with the Saints.

Patty told him: "Russell, considering that Mike hasn't left the city of Los Angeles in 90 days, and that every night he's been home in this bed by one or two in the morning, all I can say is, if he's been leaving Los Angeles in the morning, having an affair with your ex-wife in New York, and coming back home the same night, I think we should all give him a pat on the back. If he can handle that, he deserves whatever he can get."

Patty has a good sense of humor.

Russell, meanwhile, was horrified. "You mean he wasn't even out of town last weekend?"

"No," Patty said, "he was with me the entire weekend."

"Oh my God, this woman has made a *fool* out of me," Russell said. Then he apologized profusely and said good-bye.

Patty obviously wasn't mad, but that was beside the point. What if I *had* been out of town a lot? It could have started World War III.

I got a knock on my door once at three in the morning. I struggled to my bedroom window to see who was outside. It was one of my clients. His car was in my driveway. A young woman sat in the passenger seat.

I knew what he wanted. This guy lived with his girl-friend, but the lady in his car wasn't his girlfriend. He wanted to use my extra room.

What the hell was I, Motel 6? Sorry, pal. I got back in my bed, crawled beneath the covers, and hoped it was all a very bad dream.

He wouldn't give up; he began throwing rocks at my window. He was no quarterback, but he still had a respectable arm. The rocks were smashing hard off my window; I was sure one of them would break it.

But I didn't care. I took my pillow and wrapped it around my head. Finally, I heard the screech of his tires as he drove away. Before he did, the last thing I heard was the sound of him screaming at the top of his lungs on my doorstep at three in the morning:

"Mother*fucker*, I knew you when you wore tennis shoes!"

"Dear Mike:

Agents come and agents go,
Some say yes and some say no.
But to get to the point,
We didn't leave you a joint.
So as not to be rude,
We left you a lude.

                        Chuck"

3
THE MUNCIE FILE

Who the hell was ringing my doorbell? It was 2:30 in the morning.

I dragged myself groggily to the door. Through the peephole I saw Chuck Muncie.

He was one of my clients, then a running back for the New Orleans Saints. He'd been out that night in Los Angeles presumably with two prominent NFL players. The other players were perfectly coherent; they said they were looking for a safe place to drop their friend. Chuck, meanwhile, looked like hell. One guy was on the right, the other on the left; in between, Chuck had a limp arm wrapped around each of them. His glasses had slipped down around his nose, and his chin was resting on his chest. He looked about half passed out.

They shrugged at me. "Where can we put him?"

I pointed upstairs. They dragged him up to the guest bedroom, laid him in the bed, and left. Shaking my head, I climbed back into bed.

About 10 minutes later I heard noises, human ones, from the guest bedroom, and I went to check it out. Chuck was lying on his back, fast asleep, regurgitating all over himself. I ran to his bed and turned him over on his stomach. I ran downstairs and got a bucket, ran upstairs, and put Chuck's head in the bucket. He continued to vomit. When he stopped a few minutes later, I tried to wake him. He half woke up and mumbled he was fine. I went back to sleep.

When I left for work the following morning, Chuck was still asleep. When I returned home later that day, he was gone. No note, no phone call, nothing.

Over dinner that night I thought about it: here was Chuck Muncie, this famous athlete, who could have choked and died in my home. It's not the type of thing you want to tell your grandchildren.

Chuck was probably the finest running back ever to come out of California-Berkeley. He was All-American his senior year, averaged 132.7 yards per game; in 1976, the New Orleans Saints made him the third pick in the NFL draft. Chuck's future looked brilliant. He was big, fast, and tough; his raw physical abilities rivaled any runner's in the game.

What Chuck lacked was discipline. And, ultimately, ambition: he had some productive years, but he never came close to fulfilling his potential. Though he was never charged with criminal wrongdoing, Chuck was long identified with drug use.

Some years, it seemed as if half my time was spent running around after Chuck, untangling his messes. He was consistent only in his unpredictability.

One morning, I walked into my office and my secretary said Chuck had been in earlier. He hadn't said what he wanted, but he'd left me a note on my desk. It said:

Dear Mike:

Agents come and agents go,
Some say yes and some say no.

But to get to the point,
We didn't leave you a joint.
So as not to be rude,
We left you a lude.

Chuck

And there, sitting on my desk, was a Quaalude.

Chuck once purchased a home up in Alamo, a pretty little suburb in northern California. It was a great house, but he hardly ever stayed there, rarely even went up to keep an eye on it. Chuck called me one day and asked me to contact his broker and have the house put up for sale.

The broker said the real estate market up there was hot; he could easily sell Chuck's house. He said he'd go take a look at it as soon as we hung up.

An hour later he called back. "Mike, we got some problems with Chuck's place," he said.

"Like what?"

"Well, the grass in front of the house is all dead," he said.

"That's no big deal; we can reseed it easily enough."

"What else?"

He cleared his throat. "Well, Mike, I've never seen anything like it. There's a pack of wild dogs living there. I went in there, and they almost bit my damn head off."

I stifled a laugh.

"But this is the worst part. The entire house, all 4,000 square feet of it, is wall-to-wall dog shit. I mean wall to wall, Mike. If the dogs won't get you, the stink will."

I couldn't help it; I burst out laughing. But I also felt sorry for the poor guy. I promised I'd contact Chuck and see what the story was. I finally found out—and if it hadn't been Chuck, I wouldn't have believed it myself.

It seems Chuck had bought a pair of German shepherds, a male and a female, and left them alone in the house while he went away. Chuck had some friends living in Berkeley, and he'd given them some money to feed the dogs. However,

Chuck was gone longer than he anticipated, and after a while his friends would just drive by the house, jump out of the car, and toss food through the window. In the meantime, the dogs had a litter, and by the time the broker got there, they were a pack. And the house, literally, was full of shit.

Amazing but true: because the market there was so strong, the broker had the house cleaned and sold it at a profit. Chuck actually made money on the deal.

Following his rookie season, Chuck came into Los Angeles and stayed at the Bonaventure Hotel. We had some business to discuss, so I went to see him. When I walked into the room, though, I didn't see Chuck. What I saw were several of his old Berkeley pals, lying on the beds watching television. The room was littered with room service carts, wine bottles, cheese platters, half-eaten steaks. It looked like a bomb had gone off in it.

I asked where Chuck was, and his friends pointed to an adjoining door. I walked into the next room, and it was an instant replay of the first: friends and food and wine and carts all over. Still no Chuck. I didn't have to ask. I went through another adjoining door, and there was Chuck, in party room number three. I gave him a brief lecture about letting his friends freeload off him. Chuck said he didn't mind, that was what friends were for. We discussed some business, then I waded through the wreckage and left.

I got a call from the Bonaventure 12 days later. Chuck had left the hotel but had omitted a few minor details: he hadn't checked out and he hadn't paid. He had run up a bill for $7,000.

Soon after, I got another call, this time from a rental car company. They were trying to locate Chuck Muncie. I told them Chuck had gone back east; what was the problem? Well, Chuck had rented a pair of Mercedes—one for himself, another for a friend—while he'd been lodging at the

Bonaventure. And rather than return the cars when he left town, he had left them parked beneath the Bonaventure and taken a taxi to the airport. Both cars had been sitting at the Bonaventure for over a month. At $60 per car, per night, the bill was $3,600. Rough grand total, one month, hotel and cars: $10,600. Chuck, once we tracked him down, had to cough up the money.

But during those crazy years in New Orleans, Chuck could still get it done on Sundays. In four seasons there, he made All-Pro once, and in 1979 he had the first 1,000-yard rushing season (1,198) in the history of the Saints. Behind George Rogers, he's their second all-time leading rusher.

Off the field was another story. At one point, Chuck's level of irresponsibility spiralled so high that we hired one of his friends to shadow him. His name was Leon Washington. Leon was a hell of a nice guy; for a while, I took whatever commissions I was making from Chuck and just handed them over to Leon. I even made a suggestion to the Saints: put Leon on your permanent payroll—just consider it part of the cost of having Chuck Muncie on your team.

Chuck had this habit of walking into a store in New Orleans, picking out whatever merchandise he wanted, then giving the merchants a note saying they should bill the Saints. Since Chuck was a local hero, the merchants would give him whatever he wanted. I finally got a call from the Saints; they were getting all these bills, and they weren't very happy about it. When Chuck began doing the same thing in LA, I assigned the matter to Leon.

From that point on, we never saw Leon without his briefcase; it was like the damn thing was surgically attached to his hands. One day I asked him what he had in there. Checks and money. He would drive around LA paying off Chuck's bills.

Chuck and I used to fool around with boxing, at a gym by my house that had a punching bag. I'd hit the bag a few times a week; sometimes Chuck would join me when he was in town. One day Chuck suggested we have a little match in the confined area by the punching bag. Nothing serious. Three three-minute rounds, no head punching.

I should have known better than to box with a professional football player. Several months before, I'd been at the same gym with a guy named Sylvester Hicks. Sylvester was about six foot five; he used to play defensive end for the Kansas City Chiefs. Sylvester made an offer: for five three-minute rounds, I could throw all the punches I wanted at him. He wasn't even going to swing back. He just wanted to see if I could tag him.

It turned out I could, about 150 times. Sylvester kept getting low, in a crouch, and I kept showering him with blows to the back of his head. One time he showed his face, just stuck it there like a target. As hard as I could, my 200 pounds completely behind me, I nailed him flush on the nose. I guess he'd lost all the cartilage there from his football injuries; when I hit him, I could see the flesh of his nose pressing up against his cheekbones. I thought for sure he was going down. Sylvester barely moved. He just looked at me, then let out this big, deep, belly laugh. I hadn't even stunned him.

When we were done, I took my gloves off. Every one of my knuckles was dripping blood. For the next three weeks, my hands were so bruised I could barely hold a cup of coffee.

So like I said, I *should* have known better. Instead, I accepted Chuck's challenge.

I may have been a schmuck, but I was a schmuck with a strategy. The area around the punching bag was small, with hardly any space to maneuver; if I could just stay in tight, not let Chuck use his superior reach, I figured I'd be safe. And since there were no head punches, all I'd have to do was protect my body.

For two-and-a-half rounds, it worked. Chuck wasn't doing much damage because I wouldn't give him any room to wind up. With about a minute left in the final round, he got smart.

Chuck shoved me with his left arm, about three or four feet away from him. With his right, he slammed me with an uppercut and then caught me in the kidneys. My breath rushed away, and I sank to the floor. Laughing his goddamn head off, he started counting me out.

After a seven count I slowly got back up. He nailed me again in the solar plexus. Again I kissed the floor.

I can be extremely stubborn: I was determined to last the final 30 seconds. I also knew I didn't want to get hit again. I staggered back up and immediately got Chuck in a clinch. His arms were pinned tightly underneath my armpits. My breath was coming back, my eyes were clearing; I wasn't going to move. I was just going to stand there and survive the round. Just hang on for dear life.

Chuck struggled, but he couldn't get his arms loose. I thought I had him. But with about 15 seconds left, he crouched way down into a squatting position, and, since our arms were still entangled, I involuntarily went down with him. Suddenly, with his tremendous leg strength, Chuck vaulted straight up. His arms, flying loose, slammed violently into my jaw. I nearly severed my tongue, and both sides of my mouth were split. Blood was gushing all over.

If my memory serves me, it was the last time we boxed.

Chuck never bloodied Hank Stram, but he gave him plenty of headaches. After leading the Kansas City Chiefs to a pair of Super Bowls, Stram went looking for a new challenge. He got it: he became head coach of the New Orleans Saints. Stram and I became pretty good friends. We had something in common—Chuck.

Stram called me one night during the exhibition season of Chuck's rookie year.

"Jesus Christ, Mike, where the hell is Chuck?" he said.

"I don't know where he is," I said. "It's football season. *You* should know where he is."

"Well, I don't," he said. "We had a game in Minneapolis on Sunday. Chuck said his mother was there and she was sick. He asked if he could miss practice Monday so he could stay in Minnesota with her. I said okay. But now it's Tuesday, and he hasn't come back.''

I tried to contact Chuck with no success. Stram called me on Wednesday afternoon—no Chuck. Thursday morning, no Chuck. Stram said he was getting worried; maybe something had happened.

Thursday night Stram called back. Chuck had finally appeared. Stram wasn't mad anymore. Now, he said, he felt terrible. Apparently, when Chuck arrived at practice, Stram chewed him out in front of the entire team, then hit him with the largest fine in the history of the Saints. He didn't say two words to Chuck the whole practice.

After practice, though, Chuck approached him with tears in his eyes. "Coach," he said, "I'm willing to be a man and accept the fines. But I just want you to know I was on my way back to the team, and I would have been on time, but I got paged at the airport. My mother had a heart attack, and I've been at her side ever since. I'll pay the fines, but I just wanted you to know.''

"No kidding," I said, when Stram was done.

"I feel bad, Mike," Stram said. "I made him look terrible in front of his teammates. I'm going to make amends, though. I've got my secretary on the phone right now to the hospital. She's going to send Mrs. Muncie a box of chocolates. Jesus, Mike, I feel rotten over this. You think I came down too hard on him?''

"I don't know, Hank," I said. "You're his coach. You handle this however you feel appropriate.''

We hung up. An hour later Stram was on the phone again, and his mood had changed considerably.

"That son-of-a-bitch," he screamed. "I had my secretary call the hospital. There was no Mrs. Muncie staying there. I figured maybe I got the hospital wrong, so I had her call every hospital in the city. No Mrs. Muncie. So she called his mother at home. She never had any heart attack, she wasn't even sick. That son of a bitch lied to me. He had tears rolling down his cheeks. And I fell for it. Hell, I felt sorry for him."

That was Stram for you. He really liked Chuck and went out of his way to be understanding. Chuck liked Stram too; he didn't mean to drive him crazy. Chuck was just being Chuck, and Stram was an innocent bystander.

I always liked Stram myself. He was one of my favorite NFL coaches, before I met him and after. He knows that, so I don't think he'll mind this next story.

While I was in New Orleans once on business, Stram invited me to his place for a visit. I guess he was in between apartments; he was living in a hotel suite. In one room, Hank had a couple of beds, a desk, a telephone, etc. In the next room, the beds and all the furniture had been removed. They had to be, just to make room for Hank's clothes.

The room was jammed with wardrobe racks; Stram must have had at least a hundred suits, every color, style, and cut. There also must have been a hundred pairs of shoes. I was amazed. Here was this football coach who went to work in shorts and T-shirts, with the biggest wardrobe I've ever seen, male or female.

Surprisingly, Stram left New Orleans before Chuck did. Stram left after 1977, while Chuck stayed there through mid-1980, when he was traded to the San Diego Chargers. In San Diego, Chuck continued his pattern: he frequently played well but also left a trail of neglected responsibilities and thin excuses. His career ended unceremoniously in training camp of 1985 with the Minnesota Vikings.

I always liked Chuck Muncie. And I've always regretted that he didn't take greater control of his life, personally and professionally. Chuck's the kind of guy who's rarely hurt anyone but himself. I hope he's straightened himself out.

To other agents, I was some kind of joke. They spread the word that I was a fluke: Johnny Rodgers was just this wild and crazy guy who'd stuck up a gas station as a junior in college. He was irrational, that was the only reason he went with Trope. A 21-year-old agent? That's a good one.

4
"YOU'RE NOT AS STUPID AS YOU LOOK"

There wasn't any master plan, no childhood dreams. It was fate, not design, that led to my career as a sports agent.

If my father had been the final arbiter, I would have joined him in a law career and later become a partner in his firm. But I rejected that notion. I wanted to earn my success, not have it prearranged. I wanted to ascend to the top of a profession, whatever it might be, on my own merits. I didn't want to be the rich kid, spoiled, lazy, easing into his daddy's business.

I enrolled at USC as a history major, but I was a typical freshman: I'd decide what to do with my life a little later. My last two years in college, a random chain of events nudged me toward agenting. It began, oddly, with a Porsche.

I had been making a lot of noise about asserting my independence, financial and otherwise. My father was still pushing for law school; I was trying to serve notice that I had other plans. The summer before my junior year, I took a giant step backward. I sold my soul for a 911 Porsche.

I was still a kid: when I saw the car, my quest for liberation didn't seem so vital. The Porsche cost $7,000; I asked my father to cosign a loan with me. He was reluctant; I was persistent. I finally appealed to his practical side: it was a foreign car, it would retain its value. A car like that, I argued, just starts to hit its stride at 100,000 miles.

My dad agreed to sign for the loan, under one condition. He owned several investment properties. On weekends, I would have to work for him to earn the money for the monthly note. We made the deal.

I moved furniture, cleaned vacated units, painted fences. One day stands out in my mind: I was painting a fence that ran around his home. The wood was so porous that it took 15 minutes to do a single two-foot panel. I was thinking that there had to be a better way to pay for a car. But it was academic; I was still under my father's control.

I knew it was only a matter of time. As soon as I graduated from college, my financial concerns would all disappear. My degree, I knew, would immediately get me a job.

A few months later I pulled into a gas station. While the attendant was filling my car, he noticed the USC decal in my window. He disappeared for a moment, then hurried back with something in a frame. It was a diploma from USC. He'd graduated two years earlier.

That chance conversation, seemingly innocuous, had a profound impression on me. How much of a guarantee, I began to wonder, would my diploma really be? Everyone had always told me to go earn that college degree; once I did, I'd be showered with all these opportunities. Now I wasn't so sure. I had entered USC while the Vietnam War was still on. Millions wanted student deferments, so enrollments were up across the country. Jobs for all those graduates were scarce.

I made a decision: I'd start searching for a career before I graduated, to get any edge I could. Of course, I still had to determine what that career would be.

I was still considering when my Porsche died. I was driving to school when the car began to shake violently; thick black smoke started billowing from the engine. I had it towed to the dealership, where I got the revolting news: a rod had gone through the crankshaft and put a hole in the engine block. The engine was blown. To rebuild it would cost $4,000.

I was severely depressed. And terrified. I could picture my father's reaction, especially after my bit about the 100,000 miles. I called him at work, but I lost the nerve to mention the dealer's estimate. I asked him to call the car lot and speak with the dealer himself.

About 10 minutes later my father called me back. To my complete amazement, he didn't sound upset. He said he'd just spoken with the Porsche dealer. What did the guy say? I asked. He'd get to that in a minute, he answered. First, could I do him a favor?

There was a shopping bag in the cupboard by the maid's room, he said. Get the bag and bring it back to the kitchen table. I retrieved the bag, returned to the phone.

"Good," he said. "Now, I want you to go down to the Porsche dealer with that bag. Tell them to take the fucking car, put it in the bag, and throw it in the trash . . . your Porsche days are over."

As things turned out, I caught a huge break. The car was still under warranty; the dealer had to pay for the repairs. I got rid of it anyway, sold it as soon as it was fixed. I loved that car, but my independence seemed more urgent now than it ever had. I never wanted to experience that helpless feeling again, the one I got in my stomach when my father told me what to do with that paper bag.

Thanksgiving Day, my junior year, I was at a friend's house, watching Oklahoma play Nebraska on national television. It was Number One against Number Two, the biggest college game of the year. Johnny Rodgers, Nebraska's star, ran back a punt for a 72-yard touchdown. It was the most spectacular run I'd ever seen—cut and cut back, sideline to sideline, while Oklahoma looked helpless. It turned the game for Nebraska.

After Rodgers's touchdown, I tossed out a comment, joking: "Boy, I'd sure like to be his agent."

My friends all laughed. "Yeah, sure," was the general reaction. To tell the truth, I pretty much agreed with them, and for the next several months I gave it no more consideration.

In August before my senior year, getting restless about my future, I thought again about Johnny Rodgers. Like me, Rodgers was about to become a senior. Maybe I really could be his agent. The idea appealed: I could earn a good living, travel, call my own shots. I'd recently read an article that said most agents were attorneys, typically middle-aged. I wasn't a lawyer, and I was 21 years old: it would be a tremendous challenge.

I decided to do it. I flew student standby to Lincoln, Nebraska. When I got off the plane, I tried to rent a car, but I had no credit cards, and the girl behind the counter refused. When she wouldn't budge, I pulled out 10 bucks and laid it on the counter. She rented me a car.

I drove directly to the University of Nebraska, found the practice field, and grabbed a seat in the stands. As practice broke, I spotted number 20 walking off the field. He was surrounded by autograph seekers; his teammates were moving right by him into the showers. When he signed his final autograph, I hurried up to him. He thought I was another fan.

"Hi, my name is Mike Trope. I want to be your agent. I came here from Los Angeles just to talk to you."

Rodgers looked at me, dumbfounded. But he told me to hang around; he'd speak with me after his shower.

That night, we had dinner at a restaurant in Lincoln. Even among college towns, Lincoln is fanatical about its football team. The operative phrase there is "Go Big Red."

Merchants sell "Go Big Red" underwear, "Go Big Red" toilet seats, "Go Big Red" I-don't-want-to-know-what-else. One longtime Nebraska fanatic, at her behest before she passed on, had "Go Big Red" emblazoned on her tombstone.

That night, despite the fact that the football season hadn't even started, the restaurant looked like a Nebraska pep rally. Besides Johnny, several of his teammates were also having dinner at our table. Fans kept walking by to ogle the players and ask for autographs. Dinner was on the house. A local band played the Nebraska fight song.

One of the restaurant owners stood up and proudly pointed out Johnny. "Ladies and gentlemen, I want to introduce the Heisman trophy candidate for the Nebraska Cornhuskers, our own Johnny Rodgers!"

The place went crazy. When the fans finally quieted down, Johnny introduced the other players at our table. A fan got up: "Johnny, who's that gentleman sitting next to you?" The gentleman was me.

"Everybody," Johnny announced, "I would like you to meet Merlin McKeever from the Los Angeles Rams." I was five eleven, then about 185 pounds. The real McKeever was considerably larger; he played linebacker for the Vikings, Redskins, and Rams. Obviously the local fans weren't as knowledgeable about the pros as they were about college— they believed I was McKeever. Some guy in the audience screamed out, "All right, Rams!" Everybody started yelling and applauding.

After dinner, several people approached our table seeking more autographs. Including mine. First I signed Merlin McKeever. Then I started thinking, Oh my God, I'm signing someone else's name. So I put my own initials in parentheses.

When we left the restaurant, Johnny and I went back to his apartment. He grilled me for over an hour, about my background, my education, why I thought I was qualified to become his agent. I told him I had never done anything like this before, but I had no doubt whatsoever that I could get the job done. At the end of the evening, Rodgers made no commitment. But he said to keep in touch.

That initiated a dialogue that lasted for the next six months, through both of our senior years. I would call Johnny three or four times a week, fly out to watch him play in Nebraska's big games. My friends thought I was crazy, throwing away my money. My father, still hoping I'd go to law school, was equally skeptical. He wanted to know why any athlete would sign with a 21-year-old agent, still in college, ignorant of the business. He thought I was deluding myself.

It turns out I wasn't. Following his senior season, Johnny won the Heisman trophy. A short time later he made me his agent.

To this day, I'm not sure why Johnny picked me over all the other agents. He never offered an explanation, and I never asked. I do know one thing made a significant impression: I told Johnny he didn't have to sign a contract, that we would operate only on a handshake. I did that for a specific reason. I wanted it clear that I was different from other agents; I didn't have to tie him up with a piece of paper in order for us to do business. He wasn't indentured to me. At any point, if he felt my performance wasn't satisfactory, he could walk.

Securing a Heisman winner as your initial client is extraordinary, and I have to admit, I felt pretty good about myself. The other agents weren't so enamored. Despite my Heisman coup, to them I was some kind of joke. They spread the word to players that I was a fluke: Rodgers was just this wild and crazy guy who'd stuck up a gas station as a junior in college. He was irrational, that was the only reason he went with Trope. A 21-year-old agent, representing players who are older than he? That's a good one. I'd be out of the business, they charged, within a year.

Though their insults didn't faze me, they also weren't lost on me; my determination to beat them at their own game only glowed hotter. In those early days, that was by far my greatest motivation; I wanted to prove to every last fat cat in the business, in any business, that you didn't have to be 45 years old to be a success. It was a matter not of years, but of brains and balls and desire. If you had those, prosperity could come right out of college.

By the time I was 25, several of my contracts had shattered precedents, and my competition had altered its tactics. They were still hurling charges, but fluke wasn't one of them.

It was late spring, 1973, when I began negotiating my first contract. I was 22 years old, still a few months shy of my college graduation. Johnny was also 22. But we both learned, quickly, the realities of the business.

Johnny had been a first-round pick of the San Diego Chargers. While I was negotiating with Chargers owner Harland Svare, Johnny was back in Nebraska getting arrested for driving on a suspended license; he'd have to sit in jail for almost two weeks.

Somehow, Svare learned Johnny was in jail, and flew one of his aides to Nebraska. In Johnny's cell, the aide offered Johnny a $12,000 signing bonus. The figure was absurd, even in 1973, for a Heisman winner and a team's top pick. Johnny told him no, then called me.

I was annoyed for various reasons. The offer was a joke, the Chargers had tried to circumvent me, and they'd done it cheaply—while Johnny was in jail, obviously at his most vulnerable. When they'd first drafted Johnny, the Chargers had gushed about how much they wanted him, how much he would adore the city and the organization. Funny how management's attitude changed at contract time.

My irritation came from naïveté: I simply hadn't known how the business worked. That incident with the Chargers was the beginning of my education. It blared out a message:

the *game* of football bears a fundamental difference from the *business* of football. The game has well-defined rules; you follow those rules, or you get penalized. In the business, what's fair and what isn't fair is purely subjective. There is no written code. The only hard and fast rules are to try to succeed and to keep yourself in the game.

The Chargers upped their offer. They proposed a $20,000 signing bonus with a four-year deal, for a total of roughly $100,000. When I told the Chargers that wasn't enough, Svare stormed my office in an uproar. His fists clenched, shaking with anger, he kept saying that it didn't matter how much these players made; they all spent every last penny anyhow. When his tirade was exhausted, I told Svare we still wanted more money.

It was one dead end after another; what the Chargers were offering was still far below league standards. So we exercised our other option. Johnny's rights were owned by the Montreal Alouettes of the Canadian Football League. Their numbers were much shinier, and we went with them. I got Johnny a three-year contract for $300,000, one of the top deals in pro football that season.

Though it had been my first contract, I had done my homework, and entered the negotiations feeling confident. There was no sense of dread whatsoever. At the same time, I didn't feel my bargaining tactics with the Alouettes had been at all unusual. But Sam Berger, the Alouettes owner, felt differently.

"It was a terrible ordeal, a bad, bad experience," Berger later told the press. "Trope was in there talking about things I wasn't familiar with, like averaging annuities, and things that were comparatively new in football negotiations. He was very aggressive. He demanded a pound of flesh from us, and he got it."

Poor Sam. If he only knew what was coming one year later. By then Johnny and I had lost our virginity.

Johnny had a brilliant rookie season. He won Rookie of

the Year and finished second in the MVP voting. And just as important from a bargaining standpoint, Alouettes attendance both at home and on the road increased dramatically. Johnny decided, on his own, that he was worth more money than he was getting. So when the season ended, we asked Berger to renegotiate.

Over the next two weeks we met with Berger several times. A stubborn, elderly man who had made his fortune in real estate, Berger didn't part with his money easily. He kept vacillating. One afternoon he agreed to tear up Johnny's contract. That night Johnny and I had a celebration dinner. By morning Berger had changed his mind.

Angry that Berger had reneged, we decided to turn up the pressure. This was 1974, the year that the World Football League was born. It was common knowledge that the WFL was looking for marquee players like Johnny. I told Berger about a group of businessmen down in Omaha, Nebraska, who were forming a team that would soon join the WFL. I told him how badly the Nebraskans wanted Johnny, that their offer was a lot richer than his was. They would sign Johnny now, and he would jump leagues two years later, when his contract with the Alouettes expired. Not only would the Alouettes lose Johnny, but in the interim he would be a lame duck. We gave Berger a few days to mull over this new scenario. Then we paid him another visit.

Before we did, though, I drew up a contract. It was short and simplistic, but it detailed our demands: a seven-year, no-cut contract, adding up to $785,000; $450,000 more in deferred money to be paid out at $30,000 a year for 15 years after Johnny retired; a $50,000 loan up front; a $65,000 home that Johnny had already picked out; a Rolls Royce; a house in Montreal; and disability insurance. The entire deal had to be guaranteed. Even if Johnny got hurt, he'd still collect.

Johnny signed the contract before we got to Berger's office. When we walked in, I laid the contract on his desk.

Berger read it and frowned; he said he still felt Johnny's contract was fair as it stood. I reiterated Johnny's effect on attendance and reminded him about the team in Omaha. But Berger wouldn't budge, and the conversation got heated. Finally, Johnny stood up and excused himself to use the men's room.

He came back five minutes later, and the dialogue continued. Berger's phone rang; with a mild look of surprise, he said it was a long-distance call for Johnny.

"Yeah, Bobby, it's me," Johnny said into the phone. "You're kidding. The money's in escrow already? It's guaranteed? Dynamite."

Johnny listened for a moment, then continued. "Can you have a couple prepaid tickets for me and Mike waiting at the airport? Great. And tell the people in Omaha they have a deal. See ya."

Johnny hung up the phone, smiling. "Come on, Mike, let's get the hell out of Dodge. The money's in escrow down in Omaha. We can fly there tonight and close the deal."

Johnny turned to Berger, who was a pale man to begin with, but who now looked as white as new snow.

"Mr. Berger, you always told me you were going to treat me like a son and that I should respect you like a father," Johnny said. "That respect is gone now. You've shown your true colors today, Mr. Berger. The bottom line is that I don't need you anymore. The franchise in Omaha is a go, and I'm going to be part of it when my contract ends here. See you around, Mr. Berger."

I cut in, utterly bewildered, "Johnny, don't you at least want to discuss this with Mr. Berger?"

Johnny was defiant. "It's over, Mike. We're out of here."

We both stood up and started for the door. Berger, who'd been half-listening to Johnny half-eyeing our contract, got nervous.

"Now wait a minute, boys," he said. "Just where do you think you're going?"

"Forget it, Mr. Berger," I said. "It's too late. You just saved yourself a lot of money."

Berger took one last look at the contract. He sighed deeply, pulled out a pen, and hurriedly signed the contract. He flashed us both a big smile.

"Sit down, boys," he said. "I've signed the contract, which means we have a deal. You're not going anywhere. For the next seven years, you're the property of the Montreal Alouettes. This contract is signed, sealed, and delivered. Boys, my congratulations."

Berger's smile faded when Johnny replied.

"Is that your game?" Johnny said angrily. "You mean to tell me, just because you know we can get more money somewhere else, you're suddenly going to give us what we wanted in the first place? I don't know if . . ."

"Now Johnny," Berger cut in, "a deal is a deal. And we have got ourselves a deal."

Johnny paused for a long moment, shrugged, and said that Berger was right, a deal was a deal. They shook hands. Berger told Johnny that if there was any little thing he wanted, he should just ask.

Johnny asked. "Mr. Berger, you know that new Rolls Royce that's in the contract?"

"What about it, Johnny?"

"Well, I've already picked it out, and I'd like to get it today."

Berger didn't flinch. "No problem, Johnny. You go pick it up today and have the dealer call me directly. I'll take care of it."

Berger opened up a box of his favorite cigars. He handed one to me and one to Johnny. The three of us sat there smoking our fat cigars, a couple of kids in their early 20s and a 70-year-old millionaire.

Berger eyed us thoughtfully. "Boys," he said, "you're not as stupid as you look."

He shot us a crooked grin, like he knew we'd gotten the best of him and he didn't really care. At that point in his life, Berger could afford to indulge. He had his team and his wealth. And now he had Johnny.

Johnny and I were ecstatic. By the time we left Berger's

office, Johnny had gone from a three-year, $300,000 deal to seven years for $1.5 million. It made Johnny one of the highest paid players in football on either side of the border.

Now, let's take a look at this deal. On the surface: We utilized a fundamental bargaining ploy, using the money-happy new WFL as leverage against a rival league. There's nothing extraordinary there.

In reality: There was more to this negotiation than it appeared. The truth is, there was no burgeoning WFL team in Omaha. No businessmen, no escrow account, no prepaid plane tickets. No nothing. Johnny pulled a very, very fast one on Berger.

I had dreamed up the fiction about the "businessmen down in Omaha." And I was going to leave it at that. But Johnny took the ball and ran with it, and this is what I still find amazing: from the time we got into Berger's office, Johnny, completely without my knowledge, conceived the rest of the plan on his own. It was in no way premeditated; Johnny conjured it up on the spot.

You see, that phone call Johnny received was a hoax. When Johnny saw the negotiations with Berger breaking down and excused himself to go to the rest room, he actually went to a telephone and called a friend.

Johnny told his friend what was transpiring and asked him to call Berger's office. Johnny did the rest, improvising the bogus conversation about the escrow, the plane tickets, everything. I can't blame Berger for biting; when Johnny got that call, I was as startled as Berger. But I knew Johnny was up to something, so I played the straight man. It wasn't until we left Berger's office that Johnny filled me in.

Then he went to pick up his Rolls.

The NCAA rules are not the laws of the United States. They're simply a bunch of hypocritical and unworkable rules set up by the NCAA. I would no sooner abide by the rules and regulations of the NCAA than I would the Ku Klux Klan. The NCAA says breaking its rules is unethical. I say the NCAA rules are unethical.

5
TAINTED VIRGINS: COLLEGE, CARS, AND CASH

Everyone has his own pet aversion, something that makes his skin crawl.

Mine is hypocrisy.

I'm not a saint, and I'm certainly not a prude. I've made mistakes, and I have regrets, many of which I'll get to in the course of this book.

But whatever failings I have, the one thing I've never been called, even by my enemies, is a fraud. A liar. Like me or not, you know where I stand.

Yet in this business, you deal with pretension all the time. People who hide behind cosmetic images. Self-righteous imposters, with a high moral tone, but whose hands are as dirty as everyone else's. Form over substance.

Predominantly, you see it in college football.

First, let's face reality about what college football is. It's a minor league for the NFL. It's a high-powered industry, where schools and television networks make millions. Where 18-year-old recruits get plied with cash and cars and jobs they don't have to show up for. Where "student-athletes" can barely construct a coherent sentence. Where slick-talking boosters run wild and uncensored.

The whole mythology surrounding college football—i.e., amateur sport—is an illusion. It doesn't exist. As far as I'm concerned, it never has.

Most sports people have come to accept this. The NCAA, bless its puritanical heart, has not. It can't. The NCAA is the body that rules over collegiate athletics. If the NCAA ever started making colleges actually play by its rules, the whole damn structure would come tumbling down. Every major college football team in America would be on probation. On Saturday afternoons, we would all be watching women's volleyball. And the NCAA would go broke.

So the NCAA continues to delude itself and anyone else who's naïve enough to listen. It resides in a dream world, where amateur athletes do battle for nothing more than the glory of their schools. A collegiate "Leave It to Beaver."

Forget it. College football is more like *Lord of the Flies*. It's survival of the fittest: the strongest and the richest come out on top. When virtue and morality come into play, more often than not it's by coincidence.

College football, *our* college football, a business? Absolutely. You may not like that, may not feel comfortable with it, but it's a fact. For example, for appearing in last year's Citrus Bowl, each school got paid in the vicinity of $2.4 million. Bowl-bound or not, colleges pull in revenues from television, gate receipts, concession sales, and parking fees. Alumni donations pour in all year. Money like that will buy an awful lot of pompoms, also some pretty good high school athletes.

The NCAA denies this reality. So do a handful of college football coaches. They like to tell you college football is every bit as pure as in the good old days. I've got news for you: the good old days weren't so pure either.

Remember that famous old football film, *Knute Rockne, All-American*? Frank Gipp, Notre Dame's star running back, was played by Ronald Reagan. He was brave, heroic, honest. He was the embodiment of the great amateur athlete.

Well, I read an article in a well-respected historical publication about the *real* Frank Gipp. According to the article, the real Gipp was simply mortal. When he wasn't playing football, he was getting paid for working construction. He was a pool shark and a hustler. He rarely went to class, much less graduated. Eventually Gipp stopped showing up for practice and was suspended from the team. But when the Notre Dame alumni learned of his suspension, they argued so vehemently that Gipp was reinstated.

Once, at halftime of an important game, Rockne was balling out his team for its uninspired performance. He said, "Nobody wants to win here, and that includes you, Gipp." Gipp told the coach he was dead wrong. He had $500 riding on Notre Dame.

In recent years, the NCAA, numerous college coaches, certain members of the press, and others have blamed sports agents for the ills of college sports. Sports agents, they say, infiltrate college campuses. They sign players to contracts before the expiration of their college eligibility. They loan college players money. These are violations of NCAA rules. Sports agents, therefore, jeopardize the eligibility of college football players.

That's like blaming the *Titanic* on the guy who washed the deck.

I don't buy that simplistic hype from anyone, including college coaches. The late Bear Bryant once sent me a nasty, threatening letter; he was angry that one of my aides had spoken to an Alabama player before the expiration of his college eligibility. When I sent my aide to Alabama, just before the onset of this player's final season, I knew for a fact that another Alabama player, the year before, had signed with an agent midway through his senior year on the advice of an Alabama coach in another sport. Whether

Bryant knew or not, I can't say. However, I knew Bryant's history: he wasn't nearly as pristine as his letter suggested.

I wrote Bryant back and told him as much. I also told him I felt he and other athletic directors across the country should first clean their own slates before they scapegoated others. Finally, I wished the Bear a successful season, but with a stipulation: "I hope that my alma mater, USC, kicks your ass from here to China." After USC did just that, I couldn't resist: I sent the Bear a relief map of China.

I once had an irate assistant coach confront me in person. It was a brief conversation. He said, "It takes a pretty low person to risk a kid's eligibility." I told him to go to hell— I won't stand for that kind of foolishness. Anytime I hear a college coach whine about agents tampering with a player's eligibility, I pose the same question: if you make love to a woman who's had sex a hundred times, how can you risk her virginity?

It's the same principle with college athletes. Coaches risk their players' eligibility from the day they recruit them out of high school and probably a hundred times thereafter. Those players lost their purity long before they ever heard of Mike Trope.

The NCAA rules are not the laws of the United States. They're simply a bunch of hypocritical and unworkable rules set up by the NCAA. As an agent, I absolutely wasn't bound by them.

NCAA rules are meaningless. The coaches themselves, the people who are *supposed* to be bound by them, don't abide by them either. Hell, *nobody* follows the NCAA rules.

Take your top college athlete who goes through the college athletic process. He has his season tickets sold for him at well above face value. He's been recruited with every inducement you can dream of (and a few you can't). In sum, he's trampled on NCAA rules—upwards, downwards, and sideways, with the consent, knowledge, or participation of the alumni and/or the coaches—long before I ever meet

him. That type of blatant disregard makes NCAA rules a
joke, and college football a breeding ground for hypocrisy.
I've said it before: I would no sooner abide by the rules and
regulations of the NCAA than I would the Ku Klux Klan.
I'm not a member of either organization. Nor do I subscribe
to their ethics or practices.

NCAA rules are a hoax, a whitewash, perpetuated by the
organization itself and its schools. It's a facade that, up
until recent years, went largely unexamined by the nation's
sportswriters.

In 1979, I discovered firsthand just how committed even
a prestigious magazine like *Sports Illustrated* was to investigating the truth about college sports. I had called one of
the magazine's writers, angry and fed up with the deceit, the
posing, the holier-than-thou attitude of the NCAA and
many of its coaches. I told the writer about how sleazy the
recruiting process was, how players weren't going to classes
or getting an education, all those things that are common
knowledge today. As the conversation evolved, I also revealed that I was suing several athletes for breaking contracts they had signed with my firm. I was just sick and
tired of all the bullshit surrounding college football; I felt
this urge, almost a need, to depict things as they really were.

It blew up in my face. The writer conceded that I had
spoken with "astonishing candor." But what was printed in
Sports Illustrated was not an exposé of college sports. It was
an indictment of Mike Trope. It made it appear as if I,
alone, was embroiled in a scandal—a conspiracy to make
college athletes break NCAA rules. Not a word was printed
about athletes skipping classes, coaches giving payoffs to
high school players, athletes who could barely read. What
could have been a terrific story about the reality of college
football, far ahead of its time, never saw the light.

The moment I saw the article, I was certain of something
I already had suspected: the press in 1979, even a responsible magazine like *Sports Illustrated*, wasn't yet interested in

writing the truth about college athletics. Colleges across the country were stomping on NCAA rules. It wouldn't have taken Woodward or Bernstein to discover the truth; any reporter could have knocked on 10 people's doors, and five of them would have talked. But the press closed its eyes. It knew what was going on. It just didn't want to write it.

Why? I'm not an expert on the press, I don't claim to have the definitive answer. But I can speculate. To the typical sportswriter, I think rocking the boat was more trouble than it was worth. Why upset a world of which you're an integral, comfortable part? Why piss off a coach or a player whom you might be buddies with? Why jeopardize your access to the locker room by angering the very people who feed you your quotes? Why tell an adoring community that its heroes are less than saintly? In essence, why tell the entire truth, when part of it is so much easier?

The mentality changed in the eighties. Primarily, I think it was the post-Watergate syndrome—the media became much more aggressive, much less accepting—and it just took a while to trickle over to sports. I also think sportswriters became more sophisticated: they knew that the old cliché—agent as corrupter of college athletes—wasn't just overdone, it was laughably simplistic. At any rate, today's sportswriters aren't so willing to serve as propagandists for the teams they cover. There's tremendous competition for more comprehensive, investigative reporting. Indeed, detecting scandal has become downright fashionable.

But that wasn't the climate in 1979. When I spoke with *Sports Illustrated*, all I got for my honesty was a lousy reputation. Up until that time, I had been viewed by the press (and therefore the public) as a pretty decent guy. When I entered the business, the media loved it. Here was this kid, fresh out of college, making his mark in an older man's game. There was a wire photo I used to see all the time, of the press conference when Chuck Muncie signed with the New Orleans Saints. I was wearing an old, comfortable pair of loafers, and with my foot up on a desk, you could see a hole in the bottom of my shoe. Each time the photo ran, there was a caption with a similar message: here's this kid, holes in his shoes, making it. I was the underdog.

In 1977 the story got better. That was the year I represented four of the first five draft choices in the college draft, including number one Ricky Bell and number two Tony Dorsett. There was a flurry of national publicity. I was 25 years old, a whiz kid boy wonder. I could do no wrong. Sure, agents were generally disliked even then. But because I was young, because I wore jeans and old loafers, instead of fluorescent suits and gold chains, I was seen as different.

After five years in the business, I went from David to Goliath. I wasn't a novelty anymore, a college kid following a whim. To those who "knew" me only by what they read about me, I was now the establishment, the top agent in the game, whose financial success was fairly conspicuous. I was still good copy, but for a different reason. It wasn't like it had been: hey, the kid must *be* something. It was: hey, this guy must be *up* to something. The press had built me up. It was time to cut me back down.

I consider that *Sports Illustrated* article the demarcation point of my public image. Although it was a gradual process, the article was the impetus. Everybody reads *Sports Illustrated*. In fact, to this day, people still ask me about the article. And agents still use it against me. Just like an Iowa State might run down rival Iowa to a high school recruit, agents are notorious for bad-mouthing their competition while trying to sign a client. Competing agents used the *Sports Illustrated* article years after it ran to try to sway athletes from hiring me. I know this; players have told me.

The truth is, I wasn't nearly as innocent as the press first made me out to be. Nor, once the press decided I was a villain, was I remotely as evil. But after the *SI* article, my image took on a personality of its own.

It was a bunch of crap. And now that *I'm* the press, in a

manner, I'll address in proper context the topic everyone seems to want to hear about: lending players money.

Yes, I lent players money. No, it was not a majority of the players I represented. No, it was never large sums of money. More like $500 here, $1,000 there. It wasn't something I particularly liked doing; if I had wanted to be a banker, I would have gone into the banking business. When it was feasible, I would try to arrange for a bank to give the player a loan, rather than do it myself. I had enough headaches.

However, when I did lend a player money myself, I never had any problems sleeping at night. Since when is it a crime to lend somebody money?

It was also a business decision. You have to understand, I was never one of those agents who say they entered the business purely out of the goodness of their hearts, because they yearned to help poor, defenseless athletes. Yes, I felt gratified when I made a strong deal for a client, when I could help him improve the financial quality of his life. But it was hardly my only motive. First and foremost, I was a businessman, trying to succeed.

As a businessman, I had to lend players money just to survive. Players expect loans from agents. A college player would ask me for a loan, to help him get by until he turned pro. What was I supposed to say? "Sorry, I'd like to help you out, but I can't lend you a dime." If I had, I wouldn't have been in business long. The player would have moved right to the next agent. And taken the loan from him.

When I was actively agenting, out there on the streets recruiting athletes, people criticized me for playing by my own set of rules. Not true. I played by the rules I learned as I came up through the business. I played the game the same way everyone else did.

Sports Corporation of America, of which I'm chairman of the board, will not sign college players before their last college game. That's the way Gene Burrough, our president and CEO, wants to operate, and we've deferred to his wishes. That doesn't mean I've changed my personal views on the topic. I haven't; I still don't think there's anything wrong with players signing or consulting with agents before their last college game. In fact, in the time I was an agent, I would say at least 60 percent of the players who were drafted by the NFL in the first three rounds had made a commitment, in one form or another, to an agent before their senior season ended.

Just about every agent, or at least those who are successful, commits players early. They'll deny it, of course, but it's true. When I first spoke to Johnny Rodgers, the summer before his senior year, he had already been courted by literally dozens of agents.

Jack Mills is an agent based in Colorado; he used to represent Eric Dickerson, among others. Players used to tell me all the time that Mills was attacking me publicly for signing players early. Mills likes to appear as college football's great moralist, the good ol' boy who always plays it straight by the NCAA book.

But consider this: In the 1984 Orange Bowl, the University of Nebraska played the University of Miami. For Nebraska senior Dean Steinkuhler, now an offensive lineman with the Houston Oilers, the end of the game marked the conclusion of his college eligibility. The game ended near midnight, eastern standard time. In the next morning's newspapers, there were quotes from Steinkuhler saying he had hired Mills as his agent. When the press called Mills later that day for comment, he said Steinkuhler had called him at his home after the Orange Bowl game, at two in the morning, and hired him as his agent.

Wait a minute. Are you telling me Steinkuhler suddenly got this inspiration, in the middle of the night, just hours after his last college game, telling him to go with Jack Mills? If he did, how did the press get ahold of it in time to print it in the morning papers? I suppose stranger things have happened, but that explanation insults my intelligence. Nobody can tell me some kind of deal wasn't made with Steinkuhler, verbal or otherwise, prior to his final game.

For the record: In 1959, LSU's Billy Cannon won the Heisman trophy. Soon after, it was discovered that Cannon had signed a contract before the end of his senior season. Not simply an agency contract, but a pro football contract, with the general manager of the Los Angeles Rams. The general manager was Pete Rozelle. I was eight years old at the time.

I still don't think it's unethical for a college player to consult or sign with an agent before his last college game. I think it's okay if he does it as a junior; by then it's hardly too early to be thinking about a shot at the pros. An agent or a business manager or financial advisor—at least a responsible one—is in business to protect a player's self-interest. To assume that it's wrong for a player to seek an advisor before his last college game is to assume that his best interests are being looked out for by someone else, namely the school. That's a theory that colleges like to promote. It's a false theory.

Does the school cover the athlete with workman's comp insurance? No. Does it give him *any* insurance? No. Does it include him in the tremendous profits the school is making from his broken ribs and busted noses? Yes and no. During the recruiting process, when cars and money are tossed around, yes. After that—unless a player has signed some kind of secret contract with the school that assures him of remuneration throughout his four years—the answer is no. If a player gets seriously injured, and can't perform on Saturdays, will the school even blink before terminating his scholarship? In many cases, no.

When Theodore Roosevelt originally helped to get the NCAA enacted, its purpose was to provide rules that would prevent violence in sports; there had been a number of deaths in amateur games. To that extent, I think the NCAA served, and still serves, a valid purpose.

But people have this perception of a benevolent NCAA that protects these poor young lads. What the NCAA protects is its own self-interest. The rules of the NCAA are created artificially to protect the profit structure of college and pro football. I consider the collegiate system one of the greatest forms of labor exploitation in America.

Tell me: if an agent goes to a player who's still playing college football and offers to represent him, show him how he can make some money in his life, is that wrong? To me, telling a person that he can't seek advice before an arbitrary time limit, that he can't begin to determine his future value in the marketplace, that he can't begin to weigh his options—*that's* wrong. Who the hell is the NCAA to make that judgment?

The NCAA says breaking its rules is unethical. I say the NCAA rules are unethical.

I've told you what I've done. Now I'll tell you what I haven't done.

I never had a coach or a booster pimp for me. Translation: I never bought off a third party to try to get a client.

I decided from the onset of my career that I wasn't going to pay off anyone to get a player. If I was going to part with any money, I'd rather lend it to a player than leave it under a table for some booster or coach. With the exception of one bizarre incident (which I'll discuss later), I circumvented third parties completely; I went right to the players and made my deals with them.

That was the one business practice I had that distinguished me from virtually every other agent. I can't think of one prominent agent who didn't use some type of referral system, some inside track, to solicit clients. It's against NCAA rules for a coach to steer a player toward an agent in return for remuneration of any kind. That's not what

annoyed me; that's how those agents chose to compete, and
I'm as competitive as anyone. And, obviously, I have no
great respect for NCAA rules.

No, what sickened me was something else: the blatant
posturing. The same agents who swore they would never
break a rule were using coaches to get clients.

Artie Gigantino, USC defensive coordinator, handed over
players to agent Leigh Steinberg, I've been told. In 1985 I
represented Jack Del Rio, a USC linebacker. Del Rio told me
Gigantino tried to steer him to Steinberg. When that didn't
work, Gigantino went to work on Jack's father. For USC
home games, Gigantino was in charge of issuing tickets to
the players' parents. Steinberg also got his USC tickets from
Gigantino. Lo and behold, guess who happened to be
sitting next to each other at USC home games? Steinberg
and Mr. Del Rio. I can just see it: Mr. Del Rio is rooting for
Jack, and—surprise—so is Steinberg. Anyway, Jack said his
father and Steinberg became friendly, and Mr. Del Rio
urged Jack to sign with Steinberg. Jack went with me
instead.

The point is, all agents solicit college athletes; they just
do it in different ways. Steinberg, however, is one of those
agents who claims he doesn't solicit; he says he just sits
back, and the players come to him. Several years ago I
represented Steve Bono, a UCLA quarterback. Bono told me
that Steinberg, on several occasions, would wait for him in
the tunnel after UCLA games. Soliciting?

Even college head coaches steer players to agents. Today
John Robinson coaches the Los Angeles Rams. But when
Robinson was head coach at USC, he used to push players
to Howard Slusher. Slusher was Robinson's attorney, so
maybe it was simply out of friendship. In any case, in 1977,
I was sitting in Ricky Bell's hotel room at the Hula Bowl,
when he got a call from Robinson, asking him who his
agent was. Ricky said it was Mike Trope. Robinson was
dismayed; he said Ricky should have waited to speak with

Slusher. Slusher, he said, was his own attorney, and he was excellent. Robinson wanted Ricky to at least go and meet him. Ricky said, no, his mind was made up.

When it involved an agent like Slusher, compared to a Steinberg or a Mills, those maneuvers didn't bother me. Why? On the subject of soliciting clients, Slusher made no effort to misrepresent himself. I once read a Slusher quote in *Sport* magazine. He said college athletes *expect* to be recruited by agents, as an extension of the recruiting process they experienced before college; they don't feel they should have to get on the phone and seek out agents. Slusher was quoted: "He expects someone to call him and take him out to dinner, and that's the way you do it."

It's true, and everyone in the business knows it is. Slusher, unlike some of his peers, is honest enough to acknowledge it.

Next time you see a college athlete with a fast car, a wallet full of cash, a job he attends once every other Groundhog Day, it's a pretty safe bet he's met his friendly neighborhood booster.

6
MEXICAN WHORE DAY: A LESSON IN BOOSTERISM

I'm not an authority on college boosters. I always went directly to the players to make my deals, I had no reason to deal with boosters. But that doesn't mean I don't know what they're like.

Boosters are bank accounts with clothes on. They want their team to kick some ass, and they're willing to pay for it.

I may be exaggerating—but just a little bit. Some boosters are just avid fans who love their school. It's the ones who get carried away that give the rest a bad name. Boosters usually fall into one of two categories: overzealous alumni, or local businessmen who want a nice pair of season tickets to impress their clients. Often the categories blur into one: overzealous alumni who have now become local businessmen. The main function of booster groups is raising money. And while boosters have been known to fund a library or two, sports teams are what they really care about. Some of their fund-raising is done the basic way: asking for donations. At the larger schools, it's done primarily through control (designated by the school) of season tickets, which boosters often sell in conjunction with more hefty donations. Boosters don't spend many sleepless nights worrying about college administrators peeking over their shoulders. At many schools they have total autonomy.

For some boosters that isn't enough.

"We want their money," Penn State coach Joe Paterno once said, "but not their two cents' worth."

You know it ain't so, Joe. Boosters are a powerful element in college sports. Given the room to operate, boosters can hire and fire coaches, influence college presidents, demand the resignation of athletic directors.

Boosters also do much of the dirty work when it comes to recruiting. Next time you see a college athlete with a fast car, a wallet full of cash, a job he attends once every other Groundhog Day, it's a pretty safe bet he's met his friendly neighborhood booster.

I said earlier that I went through a third party only once to get a client. It was my second year in the business. There was no money involved, no payments whatsoever. The booster was the father of a friend, who was possibly going to introduce me to an athlete. It never materialized; the whole thing fell apart before I ever met the player.

I'll never forget the experience, though. Later in my career, once I'd been around awhile, there wasn't much about the business that surprised me. But this was something else, a shocking indoctrination that I've never forgotten. I was 22 years old; it showed me a lot about the business and too much about some of its inhabitants.

It was my second year as an agent, and I wanted to represent an athlete who played for a school in the Southwestern Conference. I thought of a friend I'd gone to school with at USC, whose father was a key recruiter and highly influential alumnus of the same Southwestern Conference school.

I gave my friend a call: Could his father introduce me to

the athlete? He said my timing was perfect; he was flying back to see one of the team's games in a couple of weeks. I could come along and meet his father. After that, he couldn't promise anything. I told him that would be great.

It was a road game, at another school in the SWC. We flew there from Los Angeles and drove straight to a hotel where his father had rented several rooms for a pregame party. Each room had a bathtub full of ice and beer. You could barely hear yourself above the hollering and carrying on.

My friend glanced at me with an apologetic look. "My dad is kind of a wild guy."

"Don't worry about it," I said. "My dad is kind of a wild guy too." My idea of a wild dad was someone who said "fuck" now and then.

After the game we flew back to their hometown in his father's private jet, and I accepted their invitation to stay for the weekend. The following morning the father took me on a tour of his plant. He was a wealthy man; he owned a company that grossed several hundred million dollars a year.

After the tour we took a drive. I was about to mention the player I wanted to meet, when we pulled into a liquor store. We went into the store, and I helped my friend's father carry out several cases of wine, which we put in the trunk. What, I asked, was all the wine for?

"Didn't anybody tell you about Mexican Whore Day?" he said.

Mexican Whore Day?

He laughed. "Don't worry about it. You'll learn all about it right now."

We drove to a basic, family-style restaurant and went into what appeared to be a small, separate room for parties. Seated at several tables were about twenty distinguished-looking men, fortyish, wearing expensive three-piece suits. There were also five or six younger attractive women.

It looked like a typical luncheon, except for one thing: each man, I couldn't help noticing, had either a whistle, a horn, or a bell lying near his feet. I thought it bizarre but didn't ask. There must be a reason, I supposed.

Lunch was served and eaten. When the plates were cleared away, my friend's father stood up and approached the dais. He was weaving. He'd already gotten into the wine.

"Okay, everybody," he boomed, "I'm here to read the minutes for Mexican Whore Day." That brought a roar from the men, incredulous looks from the women. "On second thought," he continued, "why don't you read them, Doug?"

Doug stood up and recited some kind of joke. I don't recall what it was, but I do remember it wasn't remotely funny. I also recall the punch line. It was "toot, toot."

At the exact moment that Doug said "toot, toot," my friend's father, who had positioned himself behind one of the women, reached over, grabbed her breasts, and squeezed them, yelling, "toot, toot!" Then, as if on cue, the men all pulled out their bells, horns, and whistles and started ringing, blowing, hooting, and hollering.

Mexican Whore Day: they did it every other week during the football season. Depending on whose turn it was, a few of the boys would invite some lady friends. Then, after lunch, they would "try to gross the women out." The whole damn thing, one of these clowns told me with a snort, was a "crackup."

After Doug sat down, there were more dirty jokes and outrageous comments. This, however, was not the end of Mexican Whore Day. Just the prelude.

When the meeting convened, my friend's father stood up again. He'd had a few more drinks. "It's Mexican Whore Day, boys," he yelled. "Anyone who wants a good time, get your asses over to my place."

I still hadn't spoken with him about the player.

When we arrived, the party had already started. It seemed that my friend's father, who was married, kept an additional apartment for his private use. Some of the men from lunch were there; so were several others I didn't recognize. My friend's father pulled me aside and started pointing out the men in the room, telling me who they were and how they made their living. They were all professionals: bankers, brokers, lawyers, accountants.

He nodded to another man. "That, my boy, is a relative of a United States senator." He paused for effect.

"These aren't lightweights, boy. They're all very influential members of the community."

The room was also filled with seven or eight women, who were serving drinks and lighting cigarettes. He didn't say who they were.

When it appeared that everyone had arrived, our host hollered at one of his buddies, "Boy," he yelled, "roll out the *weed*. Roll out the *weed*, boy."

The guy walked to a closet, came out with a shoebox, and pulled out a bag of marijuana. He rolled several joints, and a group of guys sat around and smoked them.

I, on the other hand, was preoccupied. Her name was Elaine; she was in her mid-20s, blonde and beautiful. I introduced myself, and we talked. When she excused herself to say hello to a friend, my friend's father sidled up to me. He asked me if I thought she was pretty. Hell, yes, I told him.

"Well, boy," he said, "any friend of my son is a friend of mine."

He walked over to Elaine and whispered in her ear. A moment later she came and sat down by me. We began to talk again, then she put her hand on mine. She said I should follow her. I didn't know where she was going, but I was glad to oblige.

She took me into another room, a bedroom, and we sat on the bed. She immediately started taking off her clothes. When I asked her what she was doing, she looked at me like I was insane.

"What do you mean, what am I doing?" she said. "Your

friend's daddy said I should show you a good time. That's what I'm doing."

I was flabbergasted. Also, I must admit, highly aroused. She was gorgeous to begin with; half-naked, she just wasn't playing fair.

My conscience got the best of my zipper. "Listen," I said, "you're a great-looking woman. And I'm incredibly attracted to you. But you don't have to do this if you don't want to. I don't want you to feel like someone's forcing you to do this. Why don't you just go ahead and put your clothes back on."

I guess that made sense to her; she slid back into her clothes. We sat on the bed and talked some more. She wasn't going to win any Nobel prizes, but she was nice. Kind of sweet.

Neither one of us wanted to go back to the party, and we sat on the bed and talked for about 15 minutes. I complimented her about something, she blushed and laughed, and she hugged me. Then she kissed me. Then she did a little more.

"Mike," she said, "let's get undressed . . . I want to."

Frankly, whatever reservations I'd had earlier didn't seem so monumental now. When she began undressing again, I helped her.

Just as we got into bed, the door busted open.

It was the goddamn influential members of the community.

About five of the SOBs were standing in the doorway, a couple naked, a few more in their baggy white underwear. They were bombed, bouncing up and down, shrieking, screaming for me to hurry up.

I bolted out of bed, ran to the door, slammed it in their excited faces, and locked it.

"What the hell is going on?" I gasped.

Elaine dropped her eyes, sheepish. "I guess the boys just want to have some fun," she said.

Super.

Ī scrambled into my clothes and out of the room. My friend's father stopped me in the living room. "Boy, what was going on in there? What the hell took so long?"

"Nothing," I said. "I was just talking to her."

He cringed, like I'd just confessed some heinous crime. Then he shook his head and rolled his eyes, as if he were talking to an idiot.

"You don't *talk* to a whore, boy. You *fuck* her. If every one of us was going to talk to her for half an hour, shit, we'd be here all day."

I moved past him, out the door, hopped a cab to my hotel, then another one to the airport. When my plane landed late that night, Los Angeles never seemed so calm.

That was my first encounter with high-powered boosters; I figured it was about as strange as those types of dealings could get. Then I met Sam Gilbert.

Gilbert, a millionaire contractor in Los Angeles, was the most notorious booster in UCLA history. According to an investigative series in the *Los Angeles Times*, Gilbert was, among other things, the players' all-purpose broker: "Gilbert . . . was a one-man clearing house who has enabled players and their families to receive goods and services usually at big discounts and sometimes at no cost." In the same series, former Bruin Lucius Allen said, "There were two people I listened to. Coach Wooden as long as we were between the lines. Outside the court—Sam Gilbert." Gilbert was proud of his clout and connections. People around UCLA called him "the Godfather."

My own experience with Gilbert began, indirectly, in 1973. Having recently completed the Johnny Rodgers negotiations, I was jogging one day in Westwood when I was hit in the knee by a Frisbee. I picked it up to toss it back, and standing in front of me was an extraordinarily tall, skinny, red-haired college student. It was Bill Walton, star center for the UCLA basketball team.

I introduced myself. Walton excused himself from his

game of Frisbee. He was having a great senior year, and I knew he'd soon need an agent. I told him about Rodgers and asked him if we could talk sometime. He said, "Why not now?" and invited me to his apartment where he introduced me to his girlfriend, Sue, who has since become his wife.

It was an old fraternity house that had been converted into a modest apartment building. Politically, Bill would take a much sharper left turn in later years, but I do recall a sign of what was to come. He had a dartboard with Richard Nixon's face on it.

We had a nice informal chat. We began discussing what it was like to be a college basketball player. Bill said that he was a big man and needed a lot to eat, much more than the average college student. But under NCAA restrictions, he and other players his size never had enough money to pay their food bills.

Then he told me about a man named Gilbert, a man who would come over and give him groceries. He showed me his expensive 10-speed bike and an elaborate stereo system. He said Gilbert had helped him buy those too.

I had stumbled into this, and now I was fascinated. Walton had revealed to me the inner workings of Gilbert and the UCLA basketball program. It was the first time I had heard of Gilbert.

Before leaving, I repeated that I'd like to be Walton's agent. He was pleasant but noncommittal.

I called Walton a couple of times over the next several weeks, trying to get him to go with me. He never did. He told me his agent was going to be Sam Gilbert.

What I hadn't known earlier was that Gilbert, in addition to his other services, also negotiated contracts for dozens of UCLA athletes. Not small-timers either; he'd been the agent for Kareem Abdul-Jabbar, Sidney Wicks, Curtis Rowe, and others.

I was disappointed that I didn't get Walton; he would have been a prestigious addition to my client list. Of course,

I held no grudge against Gilbert. On this one he had beaten me. That was that.

Gilbert wasn't so logical. Agents like to carve out their niche; in Gilbert's mind, UCLA was his private property. When he heard that I'd gone after Walton, he was incensed that I'd even *tried* to invade his territory.

I discovered this a short time later, after receiving phone calls from a couple of UCLA athletes I was friendly with. Their stories were identical: Gilbert had treated them to a steak dinner in Westwood, and in the course of their conversation he had warned them about this "22-year-old clip artist named Troop." He told them I had once taken an English class from his wife at Pacific Palisades High School and that she had flunked me. If this Troop guy couldn't even pass a high school English course, Gilbert ranted, then they damn sure didn't want him as their agent.

Gilbert was way out of line. I wanted him to know I was aware of what he'd done, so I decided to send him a message. What Gilbert had pulled was totally bush league. And, since he'd put on such a Mickey Mouse show, I figured he needed a Mickey Mouse cap. So I bought him one.

I took the Mickey Mouse cap and pinned a $5 bill to it. I included a note: "Dear Sam, thanks for the show. Mike Trope."

A friend's younger brother was a student at Palisades High, and I had him deliver the hat to Gilbert's wife in a paper bag, with instructions to give it to her husband. I expected to hear from Gilbert shortly. But I got no immediate response.

Some time later I received a phone call from an FBI agent; he wanted me to meet him in the bar of the Bel Air Hotel. He wouldn't tell me on the phone what he was after, but what do you say to an FBI agent? I met him at the bar. He was investigating a man named Sam Gilbert.

The FBI agent wanted my opinion: was Gilbert capable of shaving points on UCLA basketball games? I thought about that for a moment. Then I told him no.

I said: why would Gilbert, who already had such wealth, risk so much for such trivial reward? The agent responded that some people just had it in their blood; they were sick, they were in it for the thrill, not the profit. Maybe that was true, but I wasn't about to be the one to make that judgment. I was a sports agent, not a shrink. I told him I didn't even know Gilbert, not personally. I reiterated: no, I didn't think Gilbert was likely to fix UCLA basketball games.

The plot twisted again when I got a call from Richard Wood, a former USC linebacker who was then one of my clients. Richard was getting sued by, yes, Sam Gilbert. Apparently, Richard had wanted to buy a van while he was a junior at USC, and Gilbert had cosigned a loan for him. Richard never repaid it. When Gilbert sued him, Richard failed to appear in court. Now there was a judgment levied against him. Richard asked me to call Gilbert to straighten things out, and I went to his office to do so.

When I entered his office, I saw Gilbert and a large, scowling man seated on a sofa who just stared at me, offering no introduction, which I found rude and not especially comforting. Later he was introduced as Fred Slaughter, Gilbert's attorney. (Slaughter had played for John Wooden on UCLA's first national championship basketball team. Today he's an agent; one of his clients is the Lakers' Michael Cooper.)

I sat in a chair in front of Gilbert's desk. Before he spoke a word, Gilbert, a balding man in his 60s, reached into a drawer and pulled something out. It was my gift to him, the infamous Mickey Mouse cap.

Gilbert rolled up the cap in his hand. Then he threw it at me.

"Here's your *fucking* Mickey Mouse cap," Gilbert said, spitting out the words. "You can wear it a lot easier than I can. In fact, what you really need is a fucking *dunce* cap. Because that's what you are, a fucking *dunce*."

Gee, Sam, nice to meet you, too.

Needless to say, Gilbert didn't offer me a cup of coffee. He got right to the point: he charged me with going to the FBI and accusing him of point shaving. How he found out about the conversation at all, I don't know.

Although I was annoyed, I didn't show it. I calmly told Gilbert that the FBI had come to me and that I had actually defended him. Gilbert didn't believe me, so I told him again. He appeared to accept it.

Gilbert asked me why I had come to see him.

"About the money Richard Wood owes you," I said.

"Did you bring it?" he asked.

"Well, no, I thought we would discuss the terms first."

Gilbert whipped out a calculator and began feverishly punching the buttons. He looked like a mad scientist. Gilbert said the interest on the loan was accruing at something like $11.26 per day. And if I didn't pay him today, then Wood would owe him such and such a figure tomorrow.

I proposed a date by which Wood would pay back the entire sum. Gilbert agreed. That threw me off. Maybe this wouldn't get as ugly as I expected.

Wrong. I was standing to leave when Gilbert detonated.

"Don't you *ever* try and fuck me," he screamed. "You understand me? You understand what I'm saying? For *you* to try and fuck *me* is like a *mouse* trying to fuck an *elephant*.

"See, I'm a little different from most people," Gilbert yelled. "Some people, when somebody's fucking with 'em, cut their dick off. I cut off the dick *and* the balls. And everything else."

I wondered, to myself, what else there was.

"Let me tell you something else," he continued. "It is only with *great* self-restraint that I haven't had you wiped off the face of the earth. It is only with *great* self-restraint that I haven't had you killed."

He paused for venom and began again. "Don't you *ever* try and piss on me. You know what happens if you try and piss on me? It's just like trying to piss into a strong wind. The piss winds up right back in your face.''

Gilbert stopped screaming, but his intensity still charged the room. Breathless, red-faced, he literally shook with anger. Slaughter didn't look too friendly either.

Maybe, I decided, this would be a good time to go.

What would you do? I mean, there I was: a mouse trying to fuck an elephant, pissing into the wind to boot. Moreover, I liked my balls and didn't want to lose them. I was equally fond of my dick.

I said good-bye and left, but a thought kept lingering, the same one I had after "Mexican Whore Day": Who *are* these guys? And what the hell are they doing in college football?

I felt Jim Wacker blew the whistle for only one reason: to take the wind from any budding investigation. As if to say to the NCAA, we're policing ourselves at TCU; you don't have to come in here and snoop around. Once it became politically expedient, Wacker turned in his players.

7
JUST ANOTHER GUY COVERING UP

It was 1980. Kenneth Davis, high school football star from Temple, Texas, was on a recruiting trip in Fort Worth, home of Texas Christian University. He was eating pizza in a restaurant owned by Chris Farkas, a TCU booster. Mid-bite, Farkas touched Davis under the table.

"He gave me something which I stuck in my sock," Davis told *Sports Illustrated*. "I went to the bathroom to see what it was. I pulled my pants leg up, counted the money, and there was $350. I had tears in my eyes. Coming from a family of 12 children, I'd never seen that much money before. I was on cloud nine. Before leaving the bathroom I looked at myself in the mirror and said, 'I'm going to be a Horned Frog.' "

Kenneth did indeed go to TCU, where he continued the success he'd enjoyed in high school. By the end of his junior year, he was an All-American running back, a Heisman trophy candidate. But one game into his senior year, Kenneth was suspended for the remainder of his final season. He was joined on the sidelines by five of his teammates. All had accepted money, it was discovered, from TCU boosters.

Befitting a star, Kenneth had received the most. He'd been given a contract for his "services" at TCU from Fort Worth oilman Dick Lowe. Lowe and Farkas had presented it to Kenneth in a Learjet, just one day after he had signed a letter of intent to attend the University of Nebraska. Kenneth changed his mind about Nebraska, though, after he saw the magnitude of TCU's offer. Over the course of his college career, it promised Kenneth close to $38,000 in cash, goods, and payment for a nonexistent job. Lowe, at the time, was on the TCU board of trustees.

After he got suspended, Kenneth had decided to use me as his agent. He showed me his contract with Lowe. It was written like an informal memo, on yellow tablet paper. Kenneth's compensation was fully detailed, including up-front cash, signing bonuses, monthly salary, clothes, a job at Lowe's ranch, a shotgun, and a .22 caliber rifle. It was astonishing; not so much the sweetness of the deal, but the fact that such damning evidence had been put on paper. Lowe and Farkas, I concluded, never dreamed that they would get caught.

It was Jim Wacker, TCU's head coach, who blew the whistle. It was Wacker who announced the suspensions; it was Wacker who notified the Southwestern Conference and the NCAA. In the process, Wacker was lauded by many people for his "honesty," and for "cleansing the soul" of his program. Some saw Wacker as something of a martyr: by suspending six players, including its star running back, TCU would surely suffer in the win column. Wacker, they said, had made a great personal sacrifice.

I never looked at it like that.

If anyone got sacrificed, it was the TCU players. I think Wacker sold them out. And I'm sure that Kenneth Davis, though he never articulated his feelings to the public, felt the same way.

First there's the matter of Wacker's timing. At the time the TCU scandal broke, the climate in the Southwestern Conference already was turbulent. Several SWC schools were either on probation or under internal, media, or NCAA investigation. This was hardly novel: in the SWC, the most notorious conference in college football, the inmates, i.e. boosters, run the asylum.

TCU, though no improprieties had yet been made public, was not above suspicion. In 1984, TCU, a perennial loser, went to its first bowl game in 19 years. Here was a longtime doormat, in a conference infamous for cheating, suddenly a success. I don't know how the NCAA chooses which schools to investigate, but I do know that the circumstances surrounding TCU made it a ripe candidate for investigation. And it was my understanding that, even before Wacker's disclosures, the NCAA had already made its intentions known: an investigation of TCU, a fact-finding expedition at the least, was imminent.

That's exactly, I believe, what motivated Wacker to go public about TCU's transgressions. I felt Wacker blew the whistle at the precise moment he did for only one reason: to take the wind from any budding investigation. As if to say to the NCAA, we're policing ourselves at TCU; you don't even have to come in here and snoop around. Once it became politically expedient, and not until then, Wacker turned in his players.

According to Wacker, though, his timing was unavoidable and purely by chance: the players had confessed; he had no choice but to take immediate action. Wacker had conducted a team meeting the Thursday before the team's second game. In light of his team's new prosperity, and the turmoil at the other SWC schools, Wacker said he had complimented his players on improving "without breaking the rules." Following the meeting, at various intervals, Wacker said the six players confessed their wrongdoings to the coaches.

I can't speak for the suspended players. But from what

Kenneth told me, at least in his case, *confessed* wasn't quite the right word. In my opinion, *set up* would be more appropriate.

Kenneth said, yes, he'd been at Wacker's meeting. And after it broke up, he spoke with a TCU offensive coach. The coach had approached him, asking if Kenneth was still getting paid by the alumni. Kenneth told the coach he was. I asked Kenneth, already knowing the answer, why he would incriminate himself like that. He said he hadn't thought his payments were a secret—certainly not to one of his assistant coaches. That was the extent of Kenneth's "confession."

Prior to TCU's next game, he was called into Wacker's office. And informed of his suspension.

Let's suppose, for a moment, that the TCU athletes truly did confess. Does that mean that, before the so-called confession, Wacker had no idea of his program's nature? I'm sure Wacker had nothing to do with players getting paid; that was the booster's department. But I find it strange that Wacker wasn't at least *aware* that some of his players were getting compensated. Kenneth told me several TCU players were driving fancy cars around campus—parking in the athletic dorm or at practice—right under the noses of the coaches. Walker isn't blind; how could it take him so long to see the light?

Something else worth noting about the six suspended players: none were recruited by Wacker's regime, but by his predecessor's. When the story broke, we were reminded of this constantly by TCU. Does that mean that the players who confessed were the only TCU players who had broken rules? I have to doubt it. But by placing the onus squarely on those six players, it would make it clear to the world: TCU might have some bad apples, but they were picked by a former regime.

As for Wacker's great personal sacrifice, I didn't buy that either. If Wacker was so extraordinarily principled, he would have shut down the football program entirely. He would have punished *TCU*, not yanked six players off the team selectively. What kind of sacrifice did Wacker actually make? TCU lost some games it probably wouldn't have. It was also placed on probation. Meanwhile, the team kept on playing, Wacker kept on coaching, money kept rolling into the school. If Wacker's sense of ethics was so great, he would have canceled the football season. He would have sat home on Saturday afternoons and endured the same pain and humiliation the suspended players were subjected to.

I told Wacker that in person. After the suspension, Wacker did innumerable interviews. And he kept making comments to the press that I considered injurious to Kenneth's reputation. I paid Wacker a visit in Texas, and I told him what I thought. I challenged him to shut down his entire football program. Wacker was stunned; he'd been getting canonized, and now someone was actually questioning his motives. Wacker's response, in so many words, was, gee, golly, I'm just trying to do what's right. I warned him to lay off Kenneth, and I left.

What Jim Wacker did to his players, I'm convinced, was not done out of moral obligation. It wasn't the sign of sainthood, or even manhood. To me, he was just another guy covering his ass.

In retrospect, the scandal at TCU raises classic questions: Was Kenneth Davis a "victim" of the system? By accepting money to play college football, did he do something "wrong"?

I would hesitate to call Kenneth Davis a victim, since Kenneth had been paid relatively well while at TCU. The real victims aren't the players like Kenneth, the stars who get romanced, bid on, and paid. It's the little guys who get chewed up by the system. The guys who don't get paid. The guys who play for a year, get injured, and have their scholarships yanked. The guys who neglect their classes, get their heads bashed in for four years, and all to wind up with what? Little or no education, little or no shot at the pros. Those are the real victims.

But in another sense, Kenneth Davis was indeed victimized by the collegiate system. When a college gets caught breaking the rules, who gets the harshest punishment? The college? Never. Some young kid does. Kenneth, no matter what he does in the NFL, has been branded for life: "Oh yeah, the kid who took the payoffs at TCU." TCU? "Well, they're just trying to survive in the SWC."

By suspending him his senior year, Wacker took from Kenneth what he wanted most: to showcase himself for the NFL. In fact, I'd guess it was the main reason Kenneth went to college in the first place. Let's be honest about it. Like many college athletes, the education Kenneth wanted, and got, out of TCU, had nothing to do with physics and geometry. It was all about becoming a pro. By suspending Kenneth his senior year, Wacker did Kenneth an injustice. Kenneth was talented enough that he got drafted anyway, in 1986, by the Green Bay Packers. But a one-time Heisman candidate, an almost certain first-round pick, Kenneth didn't get picked until the second round. His suspension cost him a lot of cash. It cost Wacker a couple of wins.

Yeah, you might be thinking, but Davis broke the rules.

So what? Within the context of how the collegiate system works, I don't think Kenneth did anything wrong by accepting money. It was similar to having a beer during prohibition. It was illegal, but everyone did it anyway. They all knew that they were violating a law, but the law served no realistic purpose. In Kenneth's case, he didn't even break a law. Just an NCAA rule, and we already know how sacrosanct those are.

Well, he took money.

Sure he did. But first it had to be offered to him. And by men of authority—hell, a member of the TCU board of trustees. And it wasn't just at TCU. Davis also got the royal treatment at Nebraska and several other schools. Kenneth, and other kids like him, aren't blind. They immediately learn how valuable they are and how different they are from the average student when they get recruited. When a high school recruit visits a college campus, does he have to pay for his trip like a normal student would? Is he shown the library or the economics building? Is he asked if he'd like to sit in on a class or speak to a counselor?

Of course not. His airfare is paid for by the school, or maybe they bring him in on their private Learjet. He goes to parties, lavish dinners, gets set up on a date with Miss Ohio. Maybe he meets the governor, the mayor, some famous movie star who went to the school. And if he'll just agree to play football there, he's promised money, women, cars. The very people who run the show, people older and supposedly wiser, are trashing NCAA rules. To a player who's been heavily recruited, those rules become downright comical. Funnier than hell.

Once an athlete sees the system is designed to be cheated on, he's going to accept it as routine. He sees what his teammate is getting, what the guy across the conference is getting. He looks at the industry standard, then cuts the best deal he can for himself. I don't understand why this surprises people. Considering the circumstances, I don't care if you're from Manhattan or a ghetto in Louisiana— any human being is going to take what's being offered. That's not corruption. It's human nature.

Remember, these aren't payments for illegal activity. These offers are being made in return for the players' skills. They've had their brains rattled during high school for free. They get to college, the players get bigger and faster, and the beatings get worse. But now they see TV cameras, a stadium full of fans. They see dollar signs. They're getting their asses kicked. Why shouldn't they have a piece of the pie?

Affixing blame for payoffs isn't the only way in which football breeds hypocrisy. Similar posturing also surrounds the so-called student-athlete.

In 1984, I was invited to testify at California Senator

Joseph Montoya's Senate Select Committee on Licensed and Designated Sports. The topic was sports agents—how they were endangering the educational process of college athletes. The intent was to devise regulations for California agents. I accepted the invitation and flew to Sacramento. Except for Ted Steinberg, a Los Angeles attorney, I was the only agent present.

The session opened with a representative from the NFL Players Association, who ran a videotape on a television monitor. It was a halftime interview, from one of the major college bowl games. Guess who was being interviewed?

Good guess. They ran a portion of the tape where I told a broadcaster that I would not abide by NCAA rules, because, among other reasons, I didn't feel I was legally bound by them. When the tape ended, the rep from the NFLPA presented his conclusion: as long as agents had attitudes like mine, anarchy would reign in college sports. The union rep sat down, triumphant.

Speaker after speaker, that was the common thread: agents were corrupting college athletes. And as the day went on, I was getting hotter and hotter.

Finally, toward the end of the session, I was called upon to testify. At the announcement of my name, the room fell completely silent. I was waiting for someone to shout: "Enter the Christian."

First I rubbed the top of my head and assured my audience that I didn't have any horns. Then I turned to Senator Montoya. I said I was flattered to be up here at the state legislature and that I always got a kick out of seeing myself on television. Then I told the room what it didn't want to hear.

I cited USC as an example. Not because USC was any dirtier than any other school—across the board, I'd say all the major schools break the rules—but because I had gone to USC. I'd had friends who were USC athletes and had seen how they'd lived. I told the committee how I'd known players who never attended class, yet still got passing grades. Players who didn't even have to go through the tedious registration process, because others did it for them. Players who picked up brand new cars at the local dealerships. Players who had their season tickets sold, at well above face value, by assistant coaches.

I looked over at Dr. Richard Perry. Dr. Perry was then working for the NCAA, but at the time I'd gone to USC, he'd been the school's athletic director. Earlier in the day, when it was Perry's turn to speak, he'd unleashed a fiery diatribe against agents. Long on theatrics, short on facts.

I told the committee I found something disturbing: Dr. Perry, who'd been the USC athletic director at a time when academics was clearly an afterthought, would now blame agents for the poor education of college athletes. It was amazing, I said, what people might say when they had the cloak of a blue ribbon panel to hide behind.

I continued: To clean up college sports, it wasn't realistic to go after one group. It was the schools that had shirked their responsibilities. By the time a player ever met me, he either had a good education or he didn't. I had nothing to do with that. The colleges were guilty, embarrassed, looking to shift the blame. Agents made the most convenient targets.

Blaming agents, I concluded, for an illness that the schools had spread themselves, was an act of criminality.

I sat down. The room filled with uneasy whispers. I looked again at Dr. Perry. He looked like he could have drilled a hole in his seat with his ass. I was pleased at his expression, glad that I'd embarrassed him in front of the committee. For his double standards, his moral ambiguity, he deserved it.

Amazingly, the day's last few speakers portrayed me as some kind of goddamn hero. They all said how forthright and honest I was. Now they saw the truth: these kids were getting inadequate educations from the time they left high school.

At the end of the session, Senator Montoya pulled me

aside. He asked me to become a permanent member of his committee. I seemed, he said, to be the only person there who was willing to face the truth. He seemed sincere, as if he honestly wanted to help, but was just now learning what the real score was. I told him I would be honored. I'm still a member of the senator's committee.

That hearing underscores something else I find nauseating about the NCAA: its constant sermonizing about its "great contribution to American education." The fact is this: American athletes are coming out of college as functional illiterates.

Not all of them, of course. I've encountered athletes who were absolutely brilliant, who could hold their own in any intellectual capacity. On the other hand, there are far too many "student-athletes" who can barely read or write.

It isn't coincidence. The collegiate athletic system is not designed to turn around the kid who got a poor education in high school. It's designed to crank out football players. The athletes know this and respond accordingly. Kenneth Davis, I think it's fair to say, was not encouraged to pursue his education while at TCU.

I've seen other disturbing examples. One college senior wrote me a letter just before an NFL draft, informing me that I had been fired, that he'd signed with another agent. When I read his letter, I conducted an experiment. I told my eight-year-old daughter the circumstances surrounding the player's letter. I told her to write her own letter, pretending she had to fire someone. She struggled with it for five minutes, then gave it to me. I put it side by side with the letter from the player. My daughter's letter was more cohesive, her spelling more accurate.

I received another letter, from a player in the NFL who had gone to a four-year institution. Merchants were selling posters bearing his picture, without his consent; he wondered if he had grounds for a lawsuit. First he'd related his problem over the phone. Later, to remind me, he'd sent me a note. It read in part: "Please check on lawsuite fo poster."

Some years ago I negotiated a contract for an NFL rookie. Afterward, he sent me a picture of himself, with the following inscription: "I hope I become the player you except me to be."

Nebraska had been relentless, particularly its offensive coordinator. He had set up Booker with a date, given him $300 in spending money, and promised him a car. He also promised Booker that his season tickets would be sold for at least $1,000 above face value.

Nebraska's offensive coordinator, the coach who'd recruited Booker, was Tom Osborne.

8
"THE SCHOOL THAT DOESN'T CHEAT"

In the fall of 1984, the University of Nebraska got embarrassed.

Mike Rozier, their Heisman trophy winner from the season before, said in a *Sports Illustrated* article that he'd signed with an agent, and had borrowed money from him, before his last college game. In the same article Rozier also said that he'd signed a pro football contract with the Pittsburgh Maulers of the USFL before the end of his senior season.

Tom Osborne, head coach at Nebraska, was more than a little irritated. Osborne is one of the winningest coaches in America. In his 14 years as head coach, Nebraska has lost only 32 games. Every one of his teams has gone to bowl games. In the state of Nebraska, I've been told, he is second in power only to the governor.

No wonder he was so angered by Rozier's statements: about his beloved program, the only publicity Osborne seeks is the sanitized kind. Osborne is highly image-

109

conscious, expert at the dynamics of PR. He wears his purity, or at least the appearance of it, on his sleeve. Osborne likes to portray himself as the guileless leader of the squeaky-clean Cornhuskers, the School That Doesn't Cheat. The *Sports Illustrated* article caused Osborne great anxiety. It soiled NU's reputation and, by association, his own.

It was our agency Rozier was referring to. As for Rozier's contract, it was public knowledge. He received $3.1 million for three years. Not only was it guaranteed, but Rozier got more than half of that up front: $1.3 million as a salary advance and a $400,000 loan. It was one of the great deals in pro football history. As Rozier's agent, I never thought for a moment that I'd done anything less than an excellent job. Osborne, I was to discover, didn't share my sentiments.

In the winter of 1984, in the wake of Rozier's revelations, Leigh Steinberg and I were invited on the "Dick Diles Show," a nationally televised program on college football, to discuss how agents recruit college athletes. They ran a tape of Osborne standing on the sidelines of a football field, talking to a pack of reporters. He was saying he couldn't understand why Rozier had hired Mike Trope as his agent in the first place. Osborne said he had gathered all of his seniors in a room; whatever they did, he told them, there was one guy they shouldn't hire, and that was Mike Trope. He was surprised, Osborne said, that Rozier had ignored his advice.

When the tape ended, Diles and the cameras turned to me. "Well, you've just heard one of the most influential football coaches in the country speak of you as if you're a form of bubonic plague," Diles said. "Would you care to respond to that?"

I couldn't believe it. Though we'd never had any personal encounters, I knew Osborne wasn't anywhere as clean as he wanted people to believe. I knew players who'd been recruited by Nebraska—one of my assistants, Rick Panneton, had played there—and several said they were offered inducements for playing there. Osborne was no innocent.

Yet there he was on national television, ripping me, pronouncing judgment on me. Never mentioning, of course, that I had negotiated one hell of a contract for Rozier. It was a cheap shot and a terrible insult.

I told Diles yes, I would like to respond.

"Considering that I know for a fact that the University of Nebraska has violated NCAA rules by selling season tickets for their players at above face value, with the full knowledge of the coaching staff, if you could package hypocrisy and sell it, Mr. Osborne would be a multimillionaire."

That was the end of it, until several few weeks later when I attended Ricky Bell's funeral. I saw Booker Brown, a former USC lineman whom I had represented in 1974. I hadn't seen Booker for years. He'd played in the World Football League and later for the San Diego Chargers, but he'd been out of the game for the past five years. It was a tragic, emotional day, but it was comforting to see an old face. We made plans to get together.

We had lunch shortly afterward and brought each other up to date. Booker was involved in real estate in the San Fernando Valley. I told him about a project I was working on—a documentary on the recruiting experiences of college athletes. I was conducting interviews with current and former NFL players who were willing to discuss what they'd been offered by various colleges.

Booker was intrigued; he began relating his own experiences, back when he was a highly touted junior college prospect from Santa Barbara City College. Booker said the University of California–Berkeley had offered him a Grand Prix. They'd even let him test-drive it around campus. All he'd have to do was pay $200, which would be replenished by the school, and he'd receive a bill of sale just like he'd personally purchased the car. Booker said UCLA had promised him a rent-free apartment, ticket money from season tickets, and additional spending money.

But the worst experience he ever had, Booker said, was at the University of Nebraska.

Nebraska, Booker said, had been relentless, particularly

its offensive coordinator. He had set up Booker with a date, given him $300 in spending money, and promised him a car. He had also lent Booker his own car for an entire day and given him $20 for gas. And he also promised Booker that his season tickets would be sold, per season, for at least $1,000 above face value.

Nebraska's offensive coordinator, the coach who'd recruited Booker, was Tom Osborne.

Booker made a few half-joking complaints about Osborne's efforts: Booker's date hadn't been pretty, and the other schools had given him much more spending money. Then he turned serious. There was one thing Osborne had done, Booker said, that has bothered him ever since.

"Osborne put me and my mother through some changes."

Apparently, Booker said, when Osborne saw he wasn't making headway with the son, he tried to go through the mother. Osborne flew to Santa Barbara and offered Mrs. Brown six round-trip plane rides, from Santa Barbara to Nebraska, so she could see her son play football at the University of Nebraska. The airfares would all be paid for by the school, as would her lodgings.

It wasn't the bribe that upset Brown so much, but the consequences—the "changes." After Osborne's visit, Booker said his mother began insisting he go to Nebraska because that was the only school that offered *her* anything. Booker and his mother had always been close, but when he chose to go to USC, they had a nasty quarrel. For a long time, his mother remained upset.

This was getting interesting. I asked Booker if he felt strongly enough to make those statements in public. Booker said yes; the thing had eaten at him for years, for the tension it had created in his home. He said Osborne should be exposed for what he was.

Ultimately, Booker's remarks would all be recorded in my documentary. First things first, though: I sat down with

Booker and prepared a written affidavit, under penalty of perjury, specifying his charges against Osborne. Booker signed it in front of a notary public. Then we had it delivered to AP and UPI.

We didn't expect much play; the story was 10 years old, and we made no further effort to promote it. Maybe we'd get a few blurbs, at least in Lincoln or Omaha.

Boy, we were wrong. When I picked up the *Los Angeles Times* the following morning, there was Booker's picture, with his charges against Osborne. The story was also in the *Herald Examiner*. I called some friends in other cities; the papers had picked up the story there too. Booker Brown was national news.

Things began to snowball. In New Orleans, where Nebraska was preparing for the Sugar Bowl, Osborne issued a flat denial. He told reporters he had never given Booker a dime, never offered *anyone* transportation. Osborne began attacking Booker's credibility. Booker had undergone brain surgery while he was with the Chargers; he'd had a tumor removed from his pituitary gland. Osborne began insinuating to reporters that there was something wrong with Booker's mind. Booker, who'd been cool to that point, lost his temper. He told one writer that Osborne had given him the spending money after a banquet at the governor's mansion; they ate fish, and his date had buck teeth. And that if he was sane enough to remember all that, he could remember someone bribing his mother.

Up to that point, I hadn't been part of the story. But apparently someone told Osborne that I had been Booker's agent back in 1974. Osborne changed his strategy: he began suggesting that Booker had been put up to the story, that he was lying for somebody. My name began appearing in connection with the situation. It was obvious Osborne had fingered me—off the record—to the press. That was fine. Everyone's cards were on the table.

I suggested to Booker that we find a lie detection agency. It wasn't for my benefit; I already had enough proof, in my own estimation, of Booker's honesty. I sat right across from the man while he stared me in the eye and told me his story. He'd also been willing to sign an affidavit, under penalty of perjury. That was good enough for me.

Public opinion was another matter. And now Osborne, supposedly Mr. Clean, was charging Booker with lying. The lie test would put us on safer ground.

Booker went down, and they wired him up. He was asked a question regarding each specific charge against Osborne. When Booker passed his test, we sent the results to the media. He again made national news.

Osborne struck back: he took his own lie detector test and passed. I can't explain that. All I can say is, I know Booker's examiner asked specific questions; I know he told the truth about his experiences with Osborne. As for Osborne, I'm sure he also answered his questions truthfully. However, I don't know what questions he was asked or if they were specific. I never saw a copy in print.

That week, Booker got a message from Osborne, who was still in New Orleans. While I was sitting next to him, Booker called him back. Osborne said Booker's allegations weren't true; he must have forgotten what really happened. Booker said that was bullshit. He'd been recruited only once by Nebraska, and he remembered it vividly. Osborne, on the other hand, had recruited hundreds of players. It was much more likely, Booker said, that it was Osborne's memory that had lapsed.

I took the phone from Booker. I reminded Osborne of the Diles show. When, I asked, had Osborne become such an authority on what constituted an efficient agent? I'd gotten Rozier a hell of a deal, I said, and he knew it.

Yeah, Osborne said, but I'd also gotten a pretty good piece of change for that deal. Of course I had, I agreed. I got the man a $3 million deal, guaranteed, with more than half up front. Who wouldn't ask for a healthy fee on a deal like that? That's why people hired me: because I could get those kinds of contracts.

Osborne shifted gears. He said he regretted that the whole thing had ever started, beginning with the Diles show. He said that ABC had been "unethical"; they hadn't told him what he was being interviewed for. He hadn't even seen the cameras rolling because of the throng of reporters surrounding him. Had he known his comments were for national consumption, he never would have made them. He said he personally blamed ABC for the entire incident.

To me that sounded ridiculous, but I let it go. Osborne then asked me if I knew how he must feel, having to read in the newspapers that people were accusing him of being a crook. I told him yes, the same way I felt when a national TV audience heard that Nebraska players should sign with anyone—hell, sign with some janitor—but not with Mike Trope.

The conversation ended. But Booker wasn't the only one pointing fingers.

After Kenneth Davis's suspension from TCU, we had prepared an affidavit outlining what Kenneth had been paid. It also stated that several other schools had offered him financial compensation in return for his services. My intent was to convince NFL Commissioner Pete Rozelle that Kenneth shouldn't have to wait another entire year before he could turn pro, that Kenneth had simply played by the rules of the system and had already been punished enough. I wanted Rozelle to allow Kenneth to join the NFL that season, via a supplemental draft. Rozelle refused.

While I was preparing the affidavit for Rozelle, Kenneth had named Nebraska as one of his most aggressive suitors. They had treated him so royally, in fact, that he had very nearly gone to school there.

Kenneth said he'd been flown to Lincoln on a Learjet. A butler, wearing a towel over his arm, had served him cocktails and hors d'oeuvres. When he got into Lincoln, he was taken to see Osborne. They chatted, then Osborne introduced him to another Nebraska player. The player took Kenneth to meet a man, who, if Kenneth chose Nebraska, would become his "Lincoln Parent."

The man owned a mansion, Kenneth recalled, with a kitchen that was larger than Kenneth's entire home back in Temple. The man told Kenneth that, if he went to Nebraska, he would be treated like one of his sons. He took Kenneth to a stocked refrigerator; it would be open to him at any time. He took him to a separate wing of the house; if Kenneth wanted to study there, spend the night, it would be his. He took Kenneth into a five-car garage, where expensive cars were parked; if Kenneth wished, he could borrow a car whenever he pleased.

Yes, it was all against NCAA rules. No, it wasn't any greater than what the other schools had offered. But this wasn't any other school. This was Tom Osborne's Nebraska, supposedly above it all. I encouraged Kenneth to tell his story to a reporter. Unlike the Booker Brown affair, however, it received only minor press.

In early 1986, I received a telephone call from Rick Panneton, the ex–Nebraska player who once worked for me. Rick said he had to speak to me, in person, about something urgent. I asked him what it was. Rick insisted; it had to be done in person.

We met. Rick had been doing some recruiting work for Osborne; he'd been back in Lincoln shortly after Kenneth's divulgence. He said Osborne was furious that Kenneth was unearthing more dirt about his program. Osborne was certain I'd put Kenneth up to it.

Later that week, Osborne had called Rick into his office. When he arrived, Rick was surprised to see a pair of FBI agents. They wanted to know everything he knew about Mike Trope. They asked him if, while Rick worked for me, I had ever sold drugs to any athletes in his presence. They asked him if he had ever seen me doing drugs with any players. Rick told them he hadn't; I was clean. He said my only vice was money.

Rick felt I should know what was going on in Lincoln. He suggested I watch my back.

I was angry but hardly worried. I didn't care what Osborne was doing. In the area of drugs, all the coaches in America could look for as much dirt as they could possibly find, and it still wouldn't worry me. I was totally clean. Osborne could look until he passed out. There was nothing to find.

On May 21, 1986, I wasn't so nonchalant. That was the day I received a letter from the General Telephone Company. It stated:

The Public Utilities Commission of the state of California requires notification when legal process is received to release billing and/or credit information on the subscriber's account. However, when we are directed by legal process not to disclose existence of such request because there is probable cause to believe that notification to the subscriber would impede the investigation of an offense pursuant to which the legal process was issued, such notification may be deferred for an initial period of up to 90 days. This deferral can be extended to successive 90-day periods. In this particular instance, a legal referral was ordered and has now expired. Accordingly, on December 27, 1985, we received a subpoena from the U.S. District Court, District of Nebraska, for the telephone number (213) 555-7992 for the period March 24, 1982, to June 5, 1985. In response to this request, General Telephone Company of California has furnished the records to the Assistant U.S. Attorney on or about January 7, 1986. Any questions you have should be referred to the U.S. Attorney.

The letter was signed by Phillip R. Sheridan, Security

Director for General Telephone Company of California.

The phone number was not my office number. It was my home number; my home telephone records had been subpoenaed, without my knowledge, for a 3½-year period.

I had my lawyer call the U.S. Attorney's office in Nebraska. There had, in fact, been a subpoena from a Nebraska grand jury, which allowed the U.S. Attorney to obtain my telephone records. They wouldn't reveal what the intent of the investigation had been. They did say the file was marked inactive. The investigation apparently was dead.

Initially, when I first read the letter, I felt violated, almost queasy; it's a terrible sensation to know that someone can invade the privacy of your home.

After I got over that shock, I was merely livid. Why would someone have my phone records seized? To see if I was calling drug dealers, bookies, figures in the underworld? Give me a fucking break: as a businessman, I may play hard at times, but I certainly have nothing to do with that crap. Regardless, someone was determined to bury me.

The investigation had been instigated in Nebraska; I thought about my pal, Tom Osborne. True, I'm not exactly a beloved figure in that state; a lot of Nebraskans would love to see me out of business. But to involve a grand jury, it had to be someone with considerable clout. I read the letter again. I thought about what Panneton had told me, about the FBI agents in Osborne's office. I read the letter a third time. Then I picked up the phone and called Osborne.

I told Osborne my telephone records had been subpoenaed. I asked him if he knew anything about it.

Osborne didn't hesitate. He denied instigating any investigation, FBI or otherwise, into my activities. He said he had never filed charges against me in the past and had no plans to do so in the future. He conceded he was aware of an FBI investigation; he said they were scrutinizing several figures who'd come in contact with the program, in terms of their relationships with Nebraska football players. But he said he had nothing to do with it. And that, Osborne said, was all he knew.

That was the last time we spoke. In retrospect, I can only speculate on any Osborne involvement. But considering our history, the chain of events, I couldn't help envisioning an extremely powerful football coach manipulating the judicial system to try to take revenge on one of his enemies.

"One Texas coach said, 'if you go to school in Okla-homa I'll make sure you never get a job in the state of Texas in your life, if you come back to Texas.' He said, 'if you come to the University of Texas, you name five of anything, and I promise you, you'll have them by tomorrow. Anything, just five anything.'"
—Eric Dickerson

9
SPORTS CONFIDENTIAL:
THE PLAYERS TALK BACK

You've read my views on college football. Now you can read about the sport from the players themselves.

The following quotes are from *Sports Confidential*, the documentary I produced in 1985. It's never been released to the public. The only editing that's been done was for grammar, and that was minimal. Following the player's name is the college he eventually attended. Note, however, that unless a player mentions a specific college by name, he is not referring to any school in particular.

Dave Baran, UCLA: "We got a knock on the door, and there was someone standing there from Penn State that pulled up in a limo. And there was a girl hanging out the door; she was pretty sleazy. The guy approached the door, and I could tell that he was drunk. I smelled liquor on his breath, and he was very obnoxious. He had a partner with him that hadn't been drinking. They both entered my house and said they wanted to speak with me about Penn State.

Johnnie Johnson, University of Texas: "When you're 18 years old, you're a little naïve about the whole situation, and there's no way to know what the NCAA rules really are. The high school coaches try to help you out, but when everyone's coming in offering you things—from automobiles, when you may not have one at that time, to taking care of you financially—it's hard to turn that down when you're 18 years old and leaving home for the first time."

Eric Dickerson, Southern Methodist University: "Some schools offer boats, they offer houses, they'll offer $40,000. As a matter of fact, I saw $40,000. They offer cars, lifetime annuity plans, everything. They were really good at offering things to top players. Some schools would offer $1,000 just for you to come look at their campus."

Steve Bono, UCLA: "They offered a lot of money; they offered houses, cars, my high school coach a job, things like that."

Johnson: "SMU was one of my least favorite schools. They have alumni people who come in and offer you—in my case—automobiles, cash, stereo equipment, necessary things that my family might need while I was attending SMU."

Keith Stanbury, University of Oklahoma: "SMU came on at the end real strong. SMU offered me money, jobs, a Datsun 280ZX, a job working in the summertime making $10 an hour, without really working, just lifting weights. They came on real strong, and when they found out I was going to Oklahoma they added more pressure. They wanted me to come back to SMU and take another visit, which was illegal by the NCAA, and I didn't take the visit. They put a lot of pressure on me and my family."

Baran: "My mom had visited Penn State with me and went shopping with Mr. and Mrs. Paterno, had dinner with them. She enjoyed the school a lot. At the beginning of my visits she told me she was going to stay out of it. But after

According to the legend, I drove around in a long black limo brimming with prostitutes, vials of cocaine bulging from my pockets. When people meet me, they usually seem disappointed. I almost feel like apologizing: "Hey, it's my day off. The girls are in the closet."

A year after Earl Campbell signed this seven-year deal with the Oilers' owner Bud Adams, Rams' owner Carroll Rosenbloom decided he had to have Earl on his team and offered me a quarter-million dollars—cash—in a suitcase if I could arrange it.

Tony Dorsett's celebrated career as a Cowboy almost never happened; he was this close to being a Seattle Seahawk. And while Tony's had some tough times off the field—a divorce, spats with management, the outburst over Herschel Walker—he's a much better person than he's been portrayed.

Chuck Muncie thought it was hilarious that my shoes were worn, but I'm not sure it ever occurred to him that it might have been the result of trying to chase him down.

Penn State, which was my last visit, she told me she was going to get into it and tell me to go to Penn State. Well, Joe came by, and I sent my mother out, and she was gone for a while. Joe began talking about the mixed up person that I was, why I was making such a big mistake. He told me I didn't know what LA was like, I would never finish my college career, I would never play, I would never be able to graduate, I was looking for things that weren't realistic. He said I'm not keeping my parents in mind. He started talking a lot about [the fact] that I was selfish, that I wasn't thinking about my parents. That I was leaving home and my parents were getting older and they needed me. It hurt. I started to think twice about things. Here it was the day before I had to sign, and these guys are scaring me out of my decision which I had made about three or four days earlier. Well, it's a lot of pressure for a kid to deal with, especially when a guy as influential as Joe Paterno is saying things. And he was saying some pretty harsh things."

Pat Haden, USC: "In my experience there was only one school that ever offered me anything illegal. One school offered me 100 season tickets and an automobile, I believe it was."

Johnson: "I was leaning toward Texas A & M for a while until [I saw] some of their recruiting tactics. Alumni came in and persistently offered automobiles, financial support for my family, and they offered me financial support the whole time I would attend Texas A & M."

Dickerson: "When you're getting recruited, they'll totally kiss your ass. They'll give you anything you want. If you and your girlfriend want to go to Europe, anywhere you want to go, it's great, OK, sure, we can work that out. But once they get you signed, it's a little bit different. You might ask them for a favor, they'll say, recruiting's over. That's the first thing they'll tell you. Basically, that's how it goes. Some guys get caught in that trap. They asked for so much during recruiting, then after they got there, they got nothing. And some of the guys were smart: Before they signed, they'd have them draw up an agreement. You give me so much money a month, and you take care of my housing, and I want to live off campus and I want a car. They signed it, and the school would have to go by it. If not, they'd turn them into the NCAA.''

Bono: ''There were a lot of schools that offered a lot. The one that sticks out in my mind the most, though, was Temple University in Philadelphia. They had quite a bit to offer. I don't know if it was because I was a local boy, or they were trying to build their program at the time, but they were offering a lot of money, and they offered houses and cars, and my high school coach a job. It was pretty abundant.''

Baran: ''When I was being recruited by Georgia, coach [Mike] Cavan, who was Herschel Walker's coach at the time, flew into Philadelphia and drove a rent-a-car down into New Jersey and picked me up. We went to Delta Airlines, got on a plane, we got up into first class, which was illegal at the time, flew to Georgia, met with Herschel Walker. They talked about his new Trans-Am that he was driving around. They set me up with an alumni that was Jewish, because I was a Jewish athlete. They hooked me up with some guy, I forget his name, he was supposed to take care of me while I went to the university. He told me there would be no problem with finding an apartment. He said there would be no problem with transportation; they had a couple of Mercedes parked in the yard, and that I would be able to use them at any time.''

Dickerson: ''One coach told me, if he didn't get me, he'd lose his job. He cried. I mean, he literally cried in front of me. I didn't want to laugh at him, but it was funny. Because the man just cried. He said, 'if I don't get you, I'm going to lose my job. And I have a wife and kids.' I said, 'I'm sorry, you know.' ''

Bono: "Temple called one day and said to my coach, it was real close to the signing date, if you can get him to sign, we'll give him $50,000."

Dickerson: "First of all, one (Texas) coach came to my house and I told him I was going to school at the University of Oklahoma. He said, 'if you go to school in Oklahoma I'll make sure you never get a job in the state of Texas in your life, if you come back to Texas.' I was going to jump on the coach. My mom and my stepfather wouldn't let me jump on him. I said, 'get out, get the hell out.' He just kept talking, kept talking. He said, 'well, we'll talk to you some more.' He said, 'if you come to the University of Texas, you name five of anything, and I promise you, you'll have them by tomorrow. Anything, just five anything.' These are the kind of statements they make when they're recruiting."

Mike Young, UCLA: "Nebraska was probably one of the most memorable experiences I had of recruiting. The recruiting coordinator contacted me and explained that I was invited to Nebraska to attend one of their football games. In order to fly me on time, because of the fact that I had a football game the night prior to leaving for Nebraska, they were going to fly a Learjet into the airport here, and pick me up, along with two other players from Southern California. It was my first plane ride and it was quite an experience. When we arrived at Nebraska there were about 20, 25 people there to meet us. They had a small band, and donuts and coffee waiting for us. . . . There was another player from San Francisco who had also come in on a Learjet. They gave us some matches—I collect matches, so I was excited—it had the name of the aviation company, Clay Lacy Aviation, and my name embossed in gold."

Dickerson: "A NCAA guy asked me to name some schools that have NCAA violations. I named about four schools and Texas was one of them. He said, 'Texas don't have to do that.' I said, 'what do you mean?' He said, 'they're the

University of Texas.' I said, 'what the hell do you mean, they're the University of Texas?' He said, 'they're such a big university, they don't have to do that.' I said, 'the University of Texas illegally recruited me. But I can see you have a biased opinion toward the University of Texas.' And they did. They felt like Texas could do no wrong. There's schools that they overlook and Texas is one of those schools. Because they don't want to get them in trouble."

Haden: "I sold my tickets to friends and relatives, basically. It was above face value. I knew players at other schools were selling their tickets. That's not a justification for selling tickets, but it happened, and still happens, at universities all across the country."

Baran: "I would get a call from Father [Leonard] Kuberski two or three times a week. It started to bother me and my parents, because I had already known what Notre Dame was like. I was going to take a visit there already, and I didn't need anybody calling up every day."

Dickerson: "A lot of the guys on the NCAA board will never put their own universities on probation. Some of the guys on the board are from the University of Texas. Texas is never put on probation, and Texas does some things that are flat-out wrong. But they'll never be put on probation because they're UT."

Baran: "The one thing that put me in doubt about Notre Dame—even though they weren't illegal, they went by the rules—they put a lot of pressure on a 17, 18-year-old guy coming out of high school. It's tough enough to make a decision about the school and about where you want to spend four years of your life at. The problem with the pressure is that it mixes you up. You really don't know what you want. You make your mind up, but these guys are calling you and troubling you, you get all mixed up. That was one thing about Father Kuberski. He persisted in calling. He badmouthed other schools."

I spoke once with an agent who'd been to one of the bowl games. He said a group of agents had been discussing me; they were irate that I was getting the majority of top players that year. One agent raised the possibility of finding out where I was staying, and paying off the maids to plant drugs in my hotel room.

10
AGENT WARS

Theoretically, anyone can be an agent: except for California, there is no procedure for licensing. Jesse James, if he ever comes out of retirement, could be an agent.

Generally, however, agents are attorneys, seeking new clients. Just as typically, they're ruthless.

It boils down to simple math: too many agents, not enough players. Competition for clients, subsequently, gets brutal. An agent can't sign a client, or steal him, on his own qualifications. So he makes the competition look like dirt; he's bound to look better in the process. Some agents will go to any lengths, no matter how damaging, how irresponsible, to try and secure clients. It's guerilla war out there. If there are any scruples at all, they're extremely well hidden.

I was 21 years old when I entered the business; I had no idea how vicious things could get. In high school and college I'd been involved in student government; I took part in several debates. I envisioned being an agent, vying for clients, almost like a debate. One side gives its pitch, the other side offers theirs. The best side wins.

Nice ideal, but it was the same old story: the academic community, for all its virtues, bore little resemblance to the business world. And not surprisingly, the older, more jaded competition saw agenting from a completely different perspective. It was cutthroat. Some were out to destroy careers.

More than any other agent in the country, I was their primary target.

Essentially, I believe, it was my unusual success; by dominating the player pool, I was limiting other agents' potential for making money. By the late '70s, I was getting 15 to 20 blue-chip clients per season. Take 1979 for example. At one point we had 50 players signed, including 25 percent of all the players drafted in the first three rounds. Meanwhile, there were agents scrounging to get just one client. When it came to the top prospects, I wasn't among the competition, I was *the* competition. And just as a Wichita State would go after a bluechip recruit and lose it to Oklahoma, my rivals would frequently lose their prospects to me. But first, they would tear me down accordingly.

My attitude also alienated others: I clearly made it a point not to fraternize with other agents. I didn't want anything to do with them. Most of them, in my eyes, were a lying pack of hypocrites. Mea culpa; I can't sit around with enemies and pretend all's forgiven.

That included postseason bowl games and all-star games. After a few years, I just stopped going completely. Again, that turned off my competitors. They would sit around the hotel lobbies, schmoozing, commiserating, swapping war stories. By refusing to participate, I committed the unpardonable sin: I wasn't one of the boys. I was an outsider.

Postseason games were pretty gruesome anyway. They were the last chance for many agents to sign, steal, or protect clients. It was like Agent Hell; in a town like Mobile, Alabama, where they play the Senior Bowl, there would be hundreds of agents in town, more agents than ballplayers. Some agents actually used a checklist. They'd sit on the phone calling every room, trying to make their last-minute sales pitch. I'd rather have quit the business than lower myself to that level.

I sidestepped postseason games also out of a sense of survival: I didn't want some sleazy agent framing me on a drug charge; believe me, my fears were well founded. I didn't want to be in a position to be humiliated by any crook who had $20 in his pocket to buy drugs, and who figured to benefit if I was out of business. I spoke once with an agent who'd been to one of the 1979 bowl games. He said a group of agents had been sitting around discussing me one night; they were irate that I was getting the majority of top players that year. One agent raised the possibility of finding out where I was staying, and paying off the maids to plant drugs in my hotel room. If I'd been in some other occupation I might have laughed it off. As an agent, I could see it happening.

Maybe I sound paranoid. Perhaps I am, perhaps that's what being in the business did to me. If it's true, there's cause: I can't exaggerate the types of stories—stories about attacks being made on me by other agents—that used to drift back to me. There was one agent in the mid-'70s who went around claiming that my father owned a bank. The way that I really made my money, he said, was by investing my clients' money in my father's bank. Then I would keep the interest, and only give the players the principal. Mindless, right? Yet some people actually believed it. I had to run around assuring players that my father didn't own a bank, he wasn't even a stockholder in a bank. That's how ludicrous it got.

I've been told by players that an agent in Los Angeles, Steve Feldman, told them I was a drug dealer. When you went with Mike Trope, Feldman told them, he lined you up with prostitutes and took you to drug parties. The only reason I secured so many clients, Feldman charged, was by plying them with drugs and women.

That is the type of rumor that got rehashed, over and

over. I can't tell you how many times players came to me with these stories. According to my competition, I drove around in a long black limousine brimming with prostitutes, vials of cocaine bulging from my pockets. In their bizarre little fantasies, I was Mike Trope, pimp slash drug dealer.

I think I've been extremely candid about what paths I have and haven't taken during my career. Well, the one thing I never resorted to, not once, was to denigrate my competition as part of my sales pitch. I went out and sold myself. I concentrated on the positives; the types of things *we* could do for the player. If I gave a player my best shot, and he still chose another agent, I could live with it.

In return for that professional courtesy, I got zero. I must have heard the "Mike Trope rumors" at least a hundred times. From what I understand, there's only a handful of agents whose sales pitch didn't include trashing Mike Trope. One was Howard Slusher. Slusher didn't have to attack me. He was secure in his own abilities.

I've heard a million accusations, and I try to shrug most of them off. But one thing that has always infuriated me are the rumors connecting me to drugs.

For the record, these are the facts:

I don't take drugs. I have never taken drugs.

I have never furnished an athlete, college or professional, with drugs.

I have never furnished an athlete, college or professional, with a prostitute.

I had no part in the Great Train Robbery.

The image persists though, even today. I don't know whether to laugh or beat my head against the wall. When some people first meet me, they're amazed at what they see: just a regular human being with a normal appearance, not some wild-eyed, wacked-out, drug-pushing pimp. Sometimes, honest to God, they seem a little disappointed. I almost feel like apologizing: "Hey, it's my day off. The girls are in the closet."

In reality, I'm what some people would term a square. I have literally three or four drinks a year. As I was writing this book, I had the same six-pack in my refrigerator that was there four months earlier. Drugs and booze just aren't my vision of a good time. My idea of getting high is negotiating a tremendous contract, or turning around a choice piece of real estate. I also enjoy spending time with my daughters.

As for why I never got involved in drugs, it wasn't only common sense. My upbringing had a lot to do with it. My father, an attorney in Los Angeles, is a very good man. I love him. When I was a child, he also had a short, explosive temper, and not many qualms over physical punishment. My father made it plain as day: if I ever tried drugs of any kind, he would beat the holy shit out of me. As a result, I was like Pavlov's dog: if I went to a party where people were doing drugs, even smoking dope, I was out the door. It wasn't fear of the police, or my teachers. It was fear of my father. I didn't want to get my ass kicked.

That took care of any temptation I might have had as a kid. Once I got older, and understood what drugs did to people, it was a closed topic. I was too ambitious, too shrewd, too self-respecting for that kind of self-abuse.

I've heard people say: but you represented so many players who had problems with drugs. It's true, I have represented several clients who proved to have drug problems. What the hell does that have to do with me? I once had a client who was queer for sushi; personally, I can't stand the stuff.

People say, you've had twice as many clients with drug problems as other agents. Maybe, but I've also had double the clients. Show me any agent in the business—or in Hollywood for that matter—who runs a high-volume client list, who hasn't had a similar situation. It's a reality of the times.

Though my competitors never managed to mention it, the fact remains: in the course of my career, I've had clients who were made to testify in front of grand juries; players who were offered immunity if they would reveal who they received their drugs from. Did a single player say, yes, it was Mike Trope who gave them drugs? The answer is no, not once. There's a reason for that. There isn't an athlete on this earth, under penalty of perjury, who could look someone in the eye and say that I was involved with drugs.

Agent wars are waged on other fronts as well, with a variety of weapons. Let me introduce you to some of the combatants:

Witt Stewart, I found out a little too late, was a not-so-good ol' boy from Texas.

I met Stewart in Los Angeles, at a friend's wedding, at the time I represented Earl Campbell. Stewart walked up and introduced himself. He was an agent, he said, and he was very big in Texas. He could make a heap of money there for Earl in endorsements.

That sounded interesting to me. I set up a meeting between Earl and Stewart at my home. I told Stewart to make himself at home, which he did; he ate dinner at my house, raided the refrigerator, left me with some long-distance phone bills. Earl, meanwhile, felt Stewart could help him, so I had a contract drafted: Stewart would handle all of Earl's endorsements, as long as I okayed them first.

Shortly afterward, I began seeing articles in the newspapers, obviously planted by Stewart, that he was also Earl's agent for football matters. It annoyed me—I was still Earl's football agent—but I didn't bother to respond. I figured Stewart was just looking for publicity.

A few months later Earl called me. He said I was fired; Witt Stewart would now be handling him completely. Stewart was based near Houston and apparently had ingratiated himself with Earl while they were back there.

In the end, though, I got the last word. Earl eventually fired Stewart and came back to me.

International Management Group is one of the big hitters of the multiservice sports agencies. Arnold Palmer, its original client, put IMG on the map. Today, particularly in tennis and golf, IMG represents some of the country's most notable athletes.

IMG's founder and president is Mark McCormack. In 1985, McCormack wrote a popular book, *What They Don't Teach You at the Harvard Business School.* I tip my hat on one front: it's a hell of a catchy title. Too bad the message it conveys—that the McCormack book is some kind of a "street smart" guide to business—is, to me, a complete charade. In reality, it's a docile little cookbook, full of bland little recipes for success. It's about as street as Joan Collins.

I don't mention this because I'm bucking for a job as the *New York Times* book reviewer. I'm illustrating a point: I can't help feeling that McCormack's book, like his company's sanitized public image, isn't quite what it seems.

Take McCormack's reference to me, for example. McCormack wrote about one of his top executives, who went to the 1984 Orange Bowl to try to secure Mike Rozier as an IMG client. But "another agent" had already secured Rozier, with maneuvers that were less than ethical. When the "devastated" executive returned to IMG without signing Rozier, McCormack told him not to worry, that he had done well despite the results. IMG, McCormack wrote, was "not going to get down in the gutter with anyone. . . ." In short, McCormack sent one of his agents to try to sign Rozier, but the poor, virtuous fellow got done in by some brutish rival.

McCormack didn't mention me by name. He didn't have to; everyone in football knew he was referring to me. I didn't appreciate his version of the Rozier story or his book in general. It leaves a false impression: that IMG is much too high-minded to get down and dirty and compete. It's a masquerade. IMG knows the game and plays it like everyone else does.

Consider this. In the summer of 1985, I got a call from a reporter with the *Dallas Morning News.* He'd been contacted by a reporter with the *Philadelphia Inquirer*, which was doing a piece on me, and he'd asked the Dallas reporter to call me for some quotes; why he didn't call me himself, I have no idea. Shortly after, I was in Philly representing Mike Quick, when I saw a copy of the article that appeared in the *Inquirer*. The gist was that I had made myself a very rich man, while at the same time making my clients very poor. It quoted the numbers I'd received on a deal I'd made for the Cowboys' Kevin Brooks. Except that the numbers were wrong. The money was short by almost $200,000; the years were two too many. It was a major error; it made Brooks's contract seem much less substantial than it really was.

I noticed that the writer had quoted another agent, off the record. I called the *Inquirer* reporter and asked him who his source was. When he wouldn't say, I called the reporter in Dallas. He said the Philly writer's source had been an agent from IMG. It was the "devastated" agent who'd lost Rozier.

That September I was on the TCU campus, sitting in Kenneth Davis's dorm room. By then it was public knowledge that I would be representing Kenneth. The phone rang: it was IMG. Kenneth held the phone out so I could hear what the agent was saying. The guy said he'd heard rumors that Kenneth might be displeased with his representation; maybe IMG could help him. Kenneth said no, he had heard wrong, he was perfectly satisfied with Mr. Trope. The agent eventually relented; he said he'd speak again with Kenneth at another time.

Ten minutes later the phone rang again. It was someone else from IMG. He proceeded to explain in detail why I was such a poor excuse for an agent. Kenneth repeated what he'd said before.

I thought they were done then. Uh-uh. Five minutes later, the first guy was back on the phone. He was wondering: was Kenneth *sure* he was content with his agent? When Kenneth said yes, the agent reversed his field: he began telling Kenneth what a bang-up job IMG had done for a famous player in the pros. Kenneth told him he was wasting his time. He was sticking with me.

Ring. It's the famous player from the pros. He wants to know if Kenneth has any free time coming up. He has a trip planned to Europe. He sure would like to have Kenneth come with him. Kenneth politely declined.

Now, Mr. McCormack, about that gutter . . .

Everyone called Harold Daniels "The Doctor." That's because Harold told people he was a doctor. It even said so on his cards: Harold Daniels, Ph.D.

What Harold's cards didn't say was *where* he received his Ph.D. He used to say he earned it at Pepperdine, but nobody bought that. *Newsday*, in fact, reported that he got his doctorate from St. Stephen's Bible College, a correspondence school in Los Angeles. According to the college president, quoted in *Newsday*, the course load for the doctorate could be completed in a week.

Even among agents, Harold was a character. Not a bad guy, just a bit eccentric. And behind all the bullshit, Harold could also be pretty tricky.

In 1977, I had just signed Art Still, the huge defensive lineman from the University of Kentucky, now a star with the Kansas City Chiefs. I was in San Francisco—Still was playing there in the East-West All-Star game—when I got a call from Bill Alderman, one of my former aides. I told Alderman about signing Still. Alderman was confused. He had heard that Still had signed with Harold Daniels.

Still and I had a meeting. I asked him why he signed with us if he already had representation. Still shrugged and said he'd made a mistake; he had indeed signed with another agent but now wanted to stay with us. We pulled out another contract and had Still sign it.

I called Alderman, telling him the rumor he'd heard had been true, but we'd just re-signed Still. Alderman didn't say much.

The following morning there was a note in my box. It

was from Still. He was terminating the second contract.

This was getting ridiculous. I went to Still, sat him down, and signed him to another contract. The next day there was another letter in my box. It was Still, terminating us again.

I had yet *another* meeting with Still. He suggested vaguely, that someone besides Daniels was involved. But he wouldn't go any further.

I did some legwork and made a discovery: Bill Alderman was bankrolling Harold Daniels. They were partners in the same sports agency business.

Everybody tries to steal clients. Even NFL head coaches.

Actually, when Ron Meyer tried to steal my client, he was a *former* NFL head coach, having been fired by the New England Patriots. Now Meyer's back in the NFL again; he replaced Rod Dowhower as head coach of the Indianapolis Colts in December of 1986.

In the spring of 1986, though, Meyer was an agent, working for Sherwood Blount, another agent in Dallas. A few weeks before the '86 draft, Kenneth Davis paid me a visit. Although Kenneth had long ago committed to me, he told me he'd recently signed with Blount and Meyer. It was like the Still deal: Kenneth apologized and said he still wanted me as his agent.

I asked Kenneth what prompted him to sign with Meyer. He said Meyer had cosigned a hell of a car loan for him, for about $38,000. Meyer took him down to the dealership, and they picked out a car. After that, Kenneth said, he agreed to leave me and go with Meyer.

A few days after the draft, Kenneth contacted me again. Meyer wouldn't back off; Kenneth asked me to call him and explain that I was still his agent.

I phoned Meyer. "Look Ron, we'll make sure all your loans get paid back. But Kenneth would like you to get off his back."

Meyer was being cute. "I'll tell you what, Mike, I'll do the same courtesy for you. When I represent Kenneth Davis in his contract negotiations, I'll make sure all of your loans get repaid."

"Ron, you don't seem to understand this conversation. Kenneth asked me to tell you to leave him alone."

"Mike, I know. But I think in about a day or so, I'll be calling you and telling you the same thing."

This wasn't worth getting angry over. Without any rancor, I told Meyer he was out of line: he knew I had been representing Kenneth, yet he was cosigning loans for him, trying to induce him to fire me.

Finally I told Meyer to go ahead and take his best shot, and I would do the same. Kenneth ultimately stuck with me, his original agent. Meyer wound up with the Colts, working for Robert Irsay. I suppose there's some justice there somewhere.

Bud Asher was about as subtle as a punch in the groin.

In 1978, I had signed Wes Chandler, who was soon to become a rookie wide receiver with the New Orleans Saints. Wes came to me later with a familiar refrain: he had also signed with another agent. Well, Chandler said, he wasn't really an agent. He was Bud Asher, his high school football coach.

At Chandler's request, I met with Asher. I'd seen a lot of eccentric-looking agents, but nothing like this. He looked like a carnival barker: white shoes so shiny you could comb your hair in their reflection, polyester pants that could cure the blind. Above all, Asher was in perpetual heat. This was a man, I would learn, who would do virtually anything just to get a woman to have a drink with him.

Asher had a proposition. Wes seemed to like me, but Asher had known him ever since high school, so why create a problem? Asher suggested we both act as his agent. So Wes wouldn't have to pay more than the normal percentage,

Asher suggested we both cut our fee in half. Chandler was a nice kid; against my better judgment, for one deal only, Asher and I became co-agents.

Asher and I went down to New Orleans to negotiate for Wes. After three straight days with him, I can sincerely say that Bud Asher is the most obnoxious person I have ever met in my life. He certainly wasted no time ingratiating himself with the Saints: our first day in town, he tried to pick up their receptionist. After at least 60 seconds of verbal foreplay, Asher smoothly asked her to go away for the weekend. When she refused, he didn't bat an eye.

It got worse: Asher began acting as if he were the boss, and I was his peon junior partner. This was the same year I represented Earl Campbell, James Lofton, and several other first-rounders. No big deal; that's my job. But as an agent, at least give me a minimum of respect. Asher, who had never represented a player in his life, was ordering me around like I was his Steppin Fetchit.

At one point in our negotiations with the Saints, I made a comment. One comment. Asher glared at me, then asked the Saints if we could be excused. I had no choice but to follow him out.

"Now why the hell did you say that, goddamnit?" he yelled, when we were in the next room.

"I assumed, since I'm co-negotiating this contract, that I was entitled to offer my input," I said.

Asher's face reddened. We were standing in one of the Saints' meeting rooms, in front of a chalkboard. Asher picked up a piece of chalk and wrote the word *ASSUME* on the chalkboard.

"You know what happens when you assume something?" he asked.

Asher drew a vertical line after the letters *ASS*. He drew another line after the letter *U*. This left *ME*.

Asher looked back at me, triumph in his eyes. "When you assume something, you make an *ass* out of *you* and *me*."

I just stared at him. If this was a nightmare, it was awfully real.

Somehow, we reached the verge of consummating Chandler's contract. But part of the deal involved a life insurance annuity package. At the final juncture, Asher said the only way Chandler would sign was if Asher named the insurance agent. Asher's brother.

Asher was adamant: if his brother didn't sell Chandler the policy, the deal was dead. Until then, the Saints had been tolerating Asher for the same reason I had: they thought he was a little crazy. But this caused a huge row. One of the Saints' minority owners was in the insurance business; and it was club policy that any insurance policies would be purchased through his firm. Reluctantly, a compromise was hammered out; the policy would be written jointly, by both the club and Asher's brother.

Finally it was time to sign the contract. To my horror, Asher said there was one more matter we had to discuss—in private. Asher wanted $10,000 knocked off my fee. Despite our agreed-upon deal, I told Asher that was fine. By then it was worth it, just so he'd go away.

Chandler signed the contracts. It was agreed that I would collect my commission directly from the Saints. Unfortunately, however, Asher had convinced the Saints not to issue any money to anyone until a press conference the following week, when Chandler's new contract would be announced. I went to Eddie Jones, the Saints' controller, and asked him for my money right away. Jones said he wasn't sure; they were supposed to have that press conference.

I explained to Jones why I wanted my money on the spot. "I mean no disrespect to the Saints or Wes. I just don't ever want to see Bud Asher again in my life. I'll give you a break. Take a thousand bucks off my fee. The club can keep the money, as a discount for paying me one week early."

Jones, who'd also had to deal with Asher, started laughing. Then he paid me, minus the grand.

I sent one of my aides to the press conference, with a nice formal statement issued by me. Typically, I'd attend a press conference like that, but I was so tired of Bud Asher, I decided to give it a pass. The following week I received a letter from Asher. In so many words, for not showing up at the press conference, Asher said I was scum.

He could have made his point in a paragraph or two. Instead he rambled, incoherently, for seven pages. I gave the letter to my attorney. He wrote Asher back, warning him to forward any future communication through his office.

That was the first time I ever worked as a co-agent. Take a wild guess if I ever did it again.

Jerry Argovitz is an interesting study: brash, profane, combative. It was once rumored that Argovitz owned two homes—one for himself, another for his ego.

Argovitz is a former dentist who gave up root canals for real estate. He made a lot of money; in turn, he became a financial advisor. In 1980, Argovitz became a sports agent. His career was short but tumultuous.

Argovitz is a very intelligent person. But he channeled too much of his energy in the wrong direction—all he seemed to care about was beating me. Argovitz didn't give a damn what the other agents were doing. But if Mike Trope was doing anything, you could bet your life that Argovitz would try to do it better.

The thing is, if it wasn't for me, Argovitz might never have entered the business. It was one of my former aides who got Argovitz started.

In 1979, two men came to see me, Ivery Black and Gene Burrough. They had been partners in Jacksonville, Florida, in a sports agency, but they had gone broke and now were looking for work. I brought them both into my business. They went around the country selling my name.

In 1980, I received a call from Johnnie Johnson, a safety I was recruiting from the University of Texas. He told me he'd been visited in his hometown by Gene Burrough. Johnnie said Burrough had done something strange: originally, he said he was representing me. But on one of his follow-up trips, Burrough told Johnnie that Mike Trope was not the only agent who could negotiate a pro football contract. He told Johnnie he'd let him in on a secret: Burrough had actually left my organization and was now working for Jerry Argovitz. He then gave Johnnie a big sales pitch for Argovitz.

I had known that Gene and Argovitz were acquaintances. Gene's younger brother, Kenny, was a wide receiver with the Houston Oilers. Argovitz was based in Houston. Several of his clients—both when he was a dentist and when he was an investor—had been prominent Houston athletes. Argovitz and Kenny were friends; Kenny introduced Argovitz to Gene. What I didn't know was that Argovitz and Gene had gone into business.

Outside of Houston, not many people had heard of Jerry Argovitz before 1980; he had never represented any athletes. That changed drastically when Burrough went to work for him. In 1980, Gene recruited six first-round picks for Argovitz: Billy Sims, Curtis Dickey, Jacob Green, Joe Cribbs, Perry Harrington, and Cleveland Crosby. Seemingly overnight, the spotlight fell on Argovitz.

I don't mind a little competition; it keeps you sharp. But of those six first-rounders Gene had secured for Argovitz, he had initially recruited four of them while he was still working for me. My name got Gene in the door. Once he got inside, he'd make his pitch for Argovitz. Using my contacts, the credibility he had gained through working for me, Gene took my clients and handed them over to Argovitz. I used to laugh when I'd read what a super agent Argovitz was. The man got into the business on my coattails.

For the three years Argovitz was an agent, we fought a constant, heated battle for clients. Whether he admits it or not, Argovitz, it seemed to me, made it a rule to recruit the same players I did. Since both of us were after the top prospects, when it came to many of the best college players, their choice came down to me or Argovitz. Then Gene would move in. He'd say he worked for both of us, and Argovitz could do a far better job. It was effective; each year Argovitz's list expanded. In his three years in the business—though I still represented the most first-round picks—those guys were right on my tail. One year we were tied, with four first-rounders each.

Argovitz resigned as an agent in 1983. The following year he became principal owner of the USFL's Houston Gamblers. Gene Burrough, my old partner, became his general manager.

Today things have come full circle. As I mentioned, Gene is president and CEO of Sports Corporation of America. Despite all that happened, I like the man. Also, I'm a businessman. Gene is the best at what he does and has always genuinely cared about the players' best interests.

The first time I met Howard Slusher, I wasn't exactly enamored.

It was late during my first year in the business. A USC player had committed to me verbally, but he told me later that he'd also been contacted by Slusher. The player related the following story: When he told Slusher he was leaning toward me, Slusher rebuked him. Slusher said he'd be making a terrible financial blunder by signing with such a novice. On the other hand, Slusher countered, the law firm he worked for was extremely powerful. It represented President Nixon. If Slusher's firm could handle a United States president, it could clearly do great things for an athlete.

Slusher's boasts about the potency of his firm were hardly unwarranted. He practiced law for Kalmbach, DeMarco, Knapp and Schillingsworth. Herbert Kalmbach, Nixon's personal attorney on the West Coast, was also Deputy

Finance Chairman for the Committee for the Re-election of the President (CRP). During the Watergate hearings, it was revealed just how close to Nixon Kalmbach really was: he was one of Nixon's bag men. Apparently, Kalmbach had delivered suitcases full of money, from CRP's slush fund, used mainly for political sabotage. Even within Nixon's inner circle, Kalmbach was one of the few with access to the slush fund.

I didn't begrudge Slusher for tossing the weight of his firm around. It was an effective sales tool, and his claims were true. What angered me was his assertion that I wasn't qualified.

The USC player didn't seem like he really wanted to sign with Slusher. He said, however, that Slusher had made one statement that had great appeal to him: a USC alum, Slusher said his main priority was protecting the interests of USC athletes. I told the player I was concerned with his welfare too. I had a proposition: if Slusher's greatest concern was truly the player's prosperity, he could monitor my negotiations on the player's behalf. And when the deal was near completion, the player could go and get Slusher's blessing. The player agreed.

I made an appointment to go see Slusher, to see if he would agree to my proposal. I was equally eager to confront my critic.

Slusher treated me like what I was: a rookie. Not a rookie who was eager and hardworking and maybe deserved a chance. Instead, Slusher was self-important and condescending, like I was more or less a joke, a child among men, in a league I didn't belong to. Slusher finally said he would agree to my plan, with a contingency: first I would have to show him all kinds of financial statements, tax returns, corporate records. I didn't yet have those kinds of records, and Slusher knew it.

Slusher started talking about himself. He kept saying agenting was just a sideline; he had bigger things to do with his life. He told me what he told the player—that he was an agent primarily so athletes would have the finest representation available.

Having heard enough, I stood up to leave. I couldn't resist a parting shot. "Mr. Slusher, I've heard a lot of things about you. But no one ever told me how pompous you are. Have a nice day."

Slusher's ego, I suppose, stems from his accomplishments. A law graduate of USC, a Ph.D. in physical education from Ohio State, world traveler, author of a highly regarded book of philosophy, he's smart, independent, well respected. And, if you look back over the past 10 years, no one in football has had the success as sports agents that Slusher and I have had.

We have something else in common: Slusher is highly controversial, and his critics aren't difficult to locate. Much of Slusher's notoriety comes from his penchant for holding out athletes, sometimes for an entire season, over contract disputes. Fans resent him because he encourages their favorite players not to play football. Owners hate him because he's so tough.

I've orchestrated a few holdouts myself—Anthony Munoz, Kevin Brooks—but they were short, and I saw them as a final resort. It wasn't my style. As for Slusher, I think some of his holdouts were motivated, in part, by his ego. Slusher enjoys being viewed as a man with clout. I have to believe he gets a kick out of saying to an NFL owner, "Screw you, my guy will sit out if we don't get what we want." I believe there have been times when Slusher got his priorities as an agent mixed up: satisfying his ego took precedence over his clients' best interests.

Sometimes his hard line backfires. The owner says, "Go to hell, Howard Slusher. Let him sit out." Then everybody loses. Some felt it happened in 1985 with Todd Bell, a Slusher client who was an All-Pro safety for the Chicago Bears. The Bears, notoriously hard-line themselves, let Bell sit out the entire season. When the Bears won the Super

Bowl without him, not only did Bell's leverage disappear, but he missed a Super Bowl, maybe a once-in-a-career opportunity. When Bell finally returned in 1986, he couldn't even regain his starting position.

It's a two-way street, though: Slusher's tactics have also paid off with some magnificent contracts. Slusher's proven willingness to hold a player out—and his amazing ability to convince those players to sit home and withstand the heat—has made him extremely effective in negotiating salaries. When Slusher says he'll sit a guy out if he doesn't get more cash, it isn't a bluff. Slusher's one of the few agents who can put that type of fear into an NFL owner.

Though he's not particularly my kind of guy, I have great respect for Slusher's acumen as an agent. When being an agent was Slusher's top priority, when he was out there actively seeking players, there was no more fierce competitor in the business. If I had a son who was going into professional football, I'd want Slusher to be his agent.

Athletes, for the most part, are not good savers. Show me a list of the players who have become millionaires off their investments while playing pro football. Now show me a list of the players who filed for bankruptcy, who have tax liens, who are living hand to mouth.

11
GUILTY UNTIL PROVEN INNOCENT

In the past, I've rarely bothered to comment on my rivals' criticisms. First, it's a waste of time; in my business, you're damned if you do and damned if you don't.

I'll give you an example. When I negotiated contracts that included deferred income, other agents said it was a mistake because of inflation. But when I got Mike Rozier a $1 million per year contract, cash, agents pointed at his tremendous tax liability. You can't win. So why try?

Second, my competition's charges simply weren't worth dignifying. If I believed their attacks had any validity whatsoever, I would have retired from the business long ago. I would have believed I was a pimp, a drug dealer, a corrupter of college athletes, the worst thing to happen to football since bad referees.

Those are the reasons that, normally, I don't discuss other agents' accusations. However, since I've touched upon several so-called charges already, I might as well finish.

Charge: Some of my million-dollar contracts were worth considerably less because they included deferred payments.

149

This is the allegation I've heard most frequently. For instance, in *Sport* magazine in 1980, agent Tom Collins criticized the contract I negotiated for Ricky Bell. Collins claimed that kids like Ricky accepted these types of contracts because "they don't know economics."

Jerry Argovitz has also been quoted in several national publications, denigrating a contract I got for Earl Campbell, which also called for deferred income. Argovitz said his "grandmother could have done a better job for him [Earl]. And she's been dead for 10 years."

I should just consider the source, but I confess, it irritates me that people like Collins and Argovitz go on record in national publications and pass judgment on my ability as an economist. It's perfectly indicative of the kind of mindless blundering that goes on among agents to discredit their rivals.

At the time he made his claims, Collins was riding high as the business manager and agent for Kareem Abdul-Jabbar. I'm sure a lot of people accepted his comments at face value. I doubt that would be the case today. In 1986, Collins was sued for $55 million by Abdul-Jabbar for mismanagement of funds and fraud. Collins did such an inept job with his finances, Abdul-Jabbar claims in his lawsuit, that the Lakers center now can't pay off his debts. One of Abdul-Jabbar's charges is that Collins sold one of his cars and kept the money for himself. Another is that Collins had mingled the finances of several clients; in one case, he allegedly borrowed more than $200,000 from Abdul-Jabbar, without his knowledge, to pay other clients' debts. The list goes on.

There was another item worth noting in the suit against Collins. Kareem claims that Collins didn't take into account his retirement, that his income would be cut dramatically. Of course it's hindsight, but you've got to think Abdul-Jabbar would be a much happier man today if Collins had set up some type of annuity program for his retirement. Instead, Collins took money up front, which, according to Abdul-Jabbar's lawsuit, he wildly mismanaged.

To me, that's the whole point of deferred income: it gives an athlete some long-range security. It's a cushion, an insurance policy, a retirement fund for the future. And it gives a man peace of mind, no small commodity.

Let's use Ricky Bell's contract as an example. Ricky's total package came to $1.2 million, with $750,000 paid over the five years of his contract. The other $450,000 was to be paid out for 15 years, beginning when he retired. All told, it was the first million-dollar contract for a rookie in NFL history. How can you argue with that?

If you're Collins, you point to the deferred income. But putting that aside for the moment, judging Ricky's contract solely on its cash basis, it was still a nice deal. If you want to look at other agents' clients, take Lee Roy Selmon or Richard Todd. Selmon, the first player drafted in 1976, signed for $315,000 for three years. Todd, the first quarterback taken in the same draft, got $605,000 for five years. Ricky got more cash than either of them. The deferred income was gravy, like money from heaven.

Not every young player needs some type of safeguard built into his contract. And not all of my contracts included deferred money. But many of them did, for one primary reason: frugal athletes, I've found, are the exception, not the rule. Most athletes, if they have immediate, total access to all their money, are not going to make prudent investments. As for the financial advice of their agents, there aren't any Rockefellers out there in the agenting world. If there were, they wouldn't be sports agents.

I recall something the late Carroll Rosenbloom told me about his past ownership of the Baltimore Colts. Rosenbloom said he always tried to structure his players' contracts with deferred income. It made economic sense for the club, but it also protected the player. Every player who came back to the Colts and negotiated a payoff of the deferred money he was owed was, Rosenbloom said, broke within a few years. That included Johnny Unitas, who took a payoff on his deferred money, apparently made some poor investments, and later filed for bankruptcy.

As an economist, you have to look at a professional athlete differently than you would another professional. Athletes, for the most part, are not good savers. The critics say, well, why didn't you tell these guys to save their money? It's easy to tell someone to do something; having them do it is something else. If an athlete signs his name on pieces of paper without your knowledge, he's financially liable for his mistakes. You cannot protect him from either the predators or himself when he has total access to his money.

I believe that if all the players who have played in the NFL had taken half their salaries and deferred them, 90 percent of them would be better off than they are today. Show me a list of the players who have become millionaires off their investments while playing pro football. Now show me a list of the players who filed for bankruptcy, who have tax liens, who are living hand to mouth. There would be no comparison.

Charge: I collected my fees up front, even though the players didn't get all their money up front.

I'm guilty. If I had to do it all again, I'd still be guilty. Why? If I didn't take my fees up front, I had no guarantee I'd ever see them.

There were other times when I took part of my fee up front, then made an agreement with the team and the player so that the team would deduct my future payments from the player's paychecks and send them directly to me. Why did I want the team to perform this clerical function? For the same reason the NFL and the NFL Players Association have the teams deduct union dues and send them to the union directly, rather than go through the players: I didn't want to be in the collection business. I didn't want to chase after players, trying to enforce my bills. I would estimate that one of two things happens to 50 to 75 percent of agents' fees that aren't collected up front: they never get paid, or, at the minimum, they involve severe collection problems.

As a sports agent, a middleman, why should I be different from my counterparts in other fields? Life insurance salesmen, real estate brokers, car dealers receive their fees up front. In California today, the law says agents can't collect their fees up front. However, you can provide for security or collateral to ensure that you do get paid down the line. If my business had the same inherent security when I was an agent, that system would have been perfectly acceptable. It didn't, so whenever possible, I took my fees up front.

Charge: Many of my clients left me.

It's true: I've been hired and fired more than any agent in football history. But as I explained, I was not an umbrella agency for the majority of my career. I was hired only to negotiate contracts. After I negotiated a player's contract, my job was basically done. Until they needed a new contract, there was nothing else I could do for them.

Regardless, this is a charge you could level at just about any agent. Athletes change agents the way they change their socks.

I knew a player who signed with five different agents, including me, and took loans from four of them, not including me, and no one discovered it until the day of the draft. In one stroke, four different agents wound up getting fired.

Sometimes players know they're going to change agents and still try to squeeze the lame-duck agent for whatever they can get. It happened to me, with a graduating senior who said he was thinking about using my services. First I had to meet his parents; he said he didn't do anything without the approval of "Moms and Pops." His parents liked me, and I liked them. The player hired me.

A few weeks later, he called. He said his parents were in dire financial straits; if they didn't get a loan, they would lose their home. I cosigned a loan for his parents to keep their home from getting foreclosed. I didn't do it to keep the client. At that point in my career, the impact of having this player as a client, financial or otherwise, was negligible. I did it because his parents were nice people, and I wanted to help.

I also lent the player small amounts of money over the next several weeks. He said he was broke, but that once he signed with the pros he'd pay me back. Within 10 days of the draft, he called again. He had seen this gorgeous antique car and knew it wouldn't last long. Could I cosign a loan for him? About $40,000? He seemed good for it. I cosigned the loan.

Just before the draft, I received a call from a general manager I was friendly with. He said he had cards sitting on his desk, listing soon-to-be-drafted players and their agents. The player I'd cosigned the loan for had listed another agent on his card. The GM was surprised: wasn't that one of my clients?

The GM said the card was dated two weeks ago. Meaning the player had asked me for the car loan *after* he'd decided on another agent.

I thanked the GM and called the player.

"Yeah, well, I have been leaning in this other agent's direction," he said without a trace of apology. "I think these people can do more things for me. They can get me some good shoe deals. I don't want to have one agent for endorsements and a different agent for contracts. So I guess I'm going with them."

His nerve defied belief. "Why the hell did you get me to cosign a $40,000 loan for you, knowing you were going to use another agent?"

"Let me ask you a question," he said. "If I had told you I was going to use another agent, would you still have cosigned the car loan?"

Stunned, I slammed down the phone.

I was atypical: I made a lot of money as a sports agent. But I know some agents who got into the business not to get rich, but to work at something they thought would be fun. Most got disillusioned rapidly. They discovered that the contract a player signs with an agent is as worthless as toilet paper.

Often players change agents with no discernible cause. No matter how fine a job you do for your client, it all comes down to your personal relationship. And players won't hesitate to break contracts with agents because they know the agents won't sue. The public relations impact, most agents fear, would be much too costly.

No agents are immune. Look at virtually any player who's been around awhile, and they're all with different agents than they began with. Jim McMahon started off with Jerry Argovitz, then went to Steve Zucker, an agent based in Chicago. Eric Dickerson began with Jack Mills, fired him, went to Ken Norton and Jack Rodri, fired them and is now with McMahon's agent, Zucker.

If you've got a few minutes, consider Earl Campbell. He began with me, switched to Witt Stewart, had some deal with a banker and lawyer in Houston, came back to me, then didn't use an agent. Tony Dorsett was a similar case. I did his first contract. Then he brought in Don Cronson, then some other agent. The last guy couldn't get anywhere with the Cowboys, so Dorsett came back to me. After I did his contract, Dorsett changed to Witt Stewart. During his last negotiations with the Cowboys, Howard Slusher was Dorsett's agent for two days.

So, yes, I've been terminated often. I've also had my share of return business, like Campbell and Dorsett. And Lawrence Taylor. You know how that story goes.

On a percentage basis, I feel my retention rate was just about as good as that of anyone else in the business. And when you consider that I did business on a volume basis, I'd say it was probably better. You can't compare me to a guy who has five clients and keeps them all. It's like comparing a guy who bats five times in a season and bats 1.000. If I had 200 clients and got repeat business from 70 percent of them, I'm batting .700, .300 less than the other guy. But this is the bottom line: in the time I was an agent, I represented more players, and negotiated more contracts, than anyone in the business.

Steinberg said:

"Trope represents the black running backs, I tend to represent the white quarterbacks.

"Just look at the type of guys Trope represents. He takes the dumbest athletes he can find, the dumbest blacks."

12
LEIGH, YOUR HALO IS CROOKED

I can tell you exactly who initiated the rumors that I was involved with drugs.

It was Leigh Steinberg.

You're probably surprised: of all people, Leigh Steinberg? He's one of the premier agents in the business. Tony Eason, Mark Gastineau, Kenny Easley, and Ken O'Brien are just a few of his many notable clients.

But it's his image, not his client list, that separates Steinberg from the crowd. He's known as the white knight, the antithesis of modern sports agents. A Richie Cunningham in a den of Eddie Haskells.

In his dealings with the press, Steinberg perpetuates this front himself. He wants it understood that he's an altruist, a man with impeccable motives, a reluctant, guilt-ridden millionaire; not really in it for the money, but for the protection of defenseless athletes. The press, in turn, has lapped it right up. In print, other agents wear black. Steinberg sports a halo.

One item I used to read frequently regarded Steinberg's car. For all his wealth, apparently he still drove his old, trusty, beat-up Pinto. Well, one day I had to go to Steinberg's Los Angeles office. His little old car was out front, but so was his little old Mercedes. I was more amused than surprised. By then I was all too familiar with Steinberg's style.

But in my feelings toward Steinberg, that type of thing is secondary. Because several years ago, Steinberg exceeded the bounds of human decency. He exceeded even the "normal" dirty rules of the game. With premeditation, he tried to destroy my reputation and, in the process, drive me out of business.

It was 1976 when I got a phone call one morning from a Robert Weeder, a writer working on a story for *New West* magazine. Weeder was simply chatting at first about the weather and the smog in Los Angeles.

Then, from out of nowhere: "By the way, how's the drug trafficking business?"

I was stunned. This was 1976; in my life, no one, including other agents, had ever accused me of even trying drugs. Now this stranger was telling me I was a pusher.

"What the hell are you talking about?" I demanded.

"Oh, well, there's a rumor that you deal coke," Weeder said. "To players. And I'm writing this story on agents. At the very minimum, I'm going to write that there are rumors that you deal coke."

"Goddamnit, I'm telling you right now, if you print *anything* involving me with drugs, I'm going to sue your ass off, and your magazine. I don't care if you just say it was rumors. I'm going to prove that you were on notice, from me, to verify those rumors before you printed them. And when you couldn't, you went and printed them anyway. You understand that?"

While Weeder mumbled something, I got an idea.

"I'll make you a deal," I said. "Come down to Los

Angeles. Spend a couple of days with me. You can stay at my home; you can sit right next to me until I go to sleep at night. It isn't hard to tell when a person's involved with drugs. If you still think I'm the type of person who could be a drug dealer, write your story. But if you think I'm totally straight, then you tell me where you heard that rumor."

Weeder agreed, with a twist. He would name his source if he thought I was straight. But I had to promise that I wouldn't go to his source and tell him it was Weeder who revealed him. If I wanted to confront whoever was trying to nail me, I had to do it without implicating Weeder.

I agreed.

Weeder came down to LA and spent a day and a half with me. His conclusion: not only wasn't I a drug dealer, but socially, I was kind of a square.

I was practically salivating to find out who his source was. Weeder told me: it was Leigh Steinberg.

At first the name had no impact on me; Steinberg, in 1976, was still a relative unknown. Then something clicked.

"Wait a minute. Isn't that the guy who represented Steve Bartkowski?"

"Yeah, that's him," Weeder said.

I knew who Steinberg was, all right. The year before, when he had represented Bartkowski, he had come to my office seeking advice. Bartkowski was his first client; Steinberg wanted to pick my brain on the ins and outs of negotiations. He said he'd admired the work I'd done.

He had seemed like a nice enough guy, a little naïve but intelligent and anxious to learn. I spent about 20 minutes with him, answering all of his questions. Then I forgot about him.

After Weeder left, I sat down and thought about Steinberg and why he would initiate, with no provocation, such a destructive rumor. I called some associates who knew him better than I and came up with one conclusion: it could only be ambition. Steinberg saw me as an obstacle to his own success.

In the spring of that year, I had represented Chuck Muncie, the number two pick in the NFL draft. Like Muncie and Bartkowski, Steinberg had also gone to college at California–Berkeley. With his personal ties at Cal, coupled with the securing of Bartkowski the season before, Steinberg apparently had been certain he'd also get Muncie. Muncie would have made quite a plum for a young, ambitious agent. Then I came along, signed Muncie, and exploded Steinberg's plans.

That wasn't good enough for me. I didn't like losing clients either, but if another agent beat me to a player, I wouldn't go running to the press and cry that my rival was dealing drugs. Steinberg had responded recklessly and viciously to a routine aspect of the business. It was one thing to spread the rumor that my father owned a bank; it was the type of relatively harmless nonsense I expected from other agents and gave little attention to. But this offense was much more serious. Turning the other cheek was out of the question.

Before I did anything, I needed proof—independent of Weeder—that Steinberg was guilty. I called a guy I knew, Bill Alderman; he was a consummate con artist, usually game for almost anything. I also called in Rick Panneton. This would be a two-man operation.

I instructed Alderman: Call Steinberg and tell him you're a freelance writer working on a story on agents. Tell him you'll be submitting the story to *People* magazine, and you'd like Steinberg to be the focus. You'll also be accompanied by a photographer, Rick Panneton.

Alderman made the call. Steinberg said he'd be delighted to do the interview.

I gave Alderman his final instructions. He was not to steer the conversation toward drugs in any way. But if

Steinberg offered to discuss drugs and Mike Trope, Alderman should coax him to be as specific as possible.

Alderman and Panneton arrived at Steinberg's LA office. Alderman used a tape recorder for the interview, while Panneton snapped the pictures. They spoke for less than an hour.

As the interview evolved, the topic moved to other agents, and then specifically to me. First, however, Steinberg insisted that his words be off the record, that he must remain a confidential source. When Alderman agreed, Steinberg let me have it.

Steinberg told Alderman I delivered drugs to Chuck Muncie throughout Muncie's senior year. He said that was the reason I got Muncie as a client.

This is pure, unadulterated fiction—total, complete bullshit. But to Steinberg, that didn't matter. After they discussed other things, the subject turned back to me.

"Did Trope actually supply him [Muncie] with the drugs?" Alderman asked.

"He handed him the drugs," Steinberg said.

Alderman terminated the interview a few minutes later. He brought the tape to my office the same afternoon. I also received the photographs, of Alderman and Steinberg sitting around a pool (Steinberg, in his excitement at having a story in *People*, apparently hadn't noticed that Panneton was using a cheap Polaroid).

I listened to the tape alone. There was something else, something I never expected, which infuriated me further. Steinberg had attempted to characterize the differences between the type of players he represented and those I represented. I could not believe my ears.

Steinberg said:

"Trope represents the black running backs, I tend to represent the white quarterbacks."

"Just look at the type of guys Trope represents. He takes the dumbest athletes he can find, the dumbest blacks. . . ."

"Imagine going to a Harvard kid with white parents and trying to offer him money."

After I listened to the tape, I drove over to my father's law office and informed him of what Steinberg had done. An attorney there shot off a messengered letter to Steinberg. It stated basically: "We have been informed that you have spread malicious rumors about our client, Mike Trope. Specifically, that Trope supplied Chuck Muncie with drugs."

There wasn't any mention of the tape.

Steinberg immediately messengered back a letter of his own. He wrote that as an alumni of Cal–Berkeley, he would never discredit Chuck Muncie or the school. And that he had met Mike Trope only on one occasion and would never instigate such rumors.

It was time to stop playing games. My attorney wrote to Steinberg and informed him of our facts and witnesses. The letter also told Steinberg we knew he'd spread the same "information" to other members of the media. And that by issuing these charges anonymously—off the record—he was trying to create the impression that more than one person was accusing me of dealing drugs. In short, that he was trying to ruin my career and defame me.

Steinberg called: he wanted to come in and speak with me. I told my secretary to make an appointment.

When Steinberg arrived at my office, I was in a conference room with a pair of attorneys. Steinberg walked in. "I'd like to speak with Mike alone," he said.

I asked the attorneys to leave the room, then stared a moment at Steinberg. "Well, Leigh, what have you got to say for yourself? This is a serious thing you've done."

Steinberg took a deep breath and shifted in his seat. When he started to speak, the words got caught in his throat. Finally, he looked away and started sobbing.

When Steinberg composed himself, he said there was no excuse for what he'd done. He had gotten carried away, he said, with the competitiveness of the business. If I would let him off the hook, forget the whole affair had ever happened, he would never cross my path again or do anything else to hurt me as long as he lived.

Damn, his reaction had caught me off guard. I thought about what he'd said. I told him I'd agree: as far as I was concerned, it was history.

"But you have to understand something," I said. "What you did goes well beyond being competitive. You were putting me in a situation where my reputation could be destroyed, where people would be walking around saying I'm a drug dealer. It's over. But don't ever pull that kind of shit again."

When Steinberg assured me he wouldn't, there was nothing else to say. I said good-bye and he walked out the door.

That was the end of the Leigh Steinberg episode; I took no further action. I was still hot, but any urge I'd had for revenge was tempered by compassion; during that scene in my office, he'd been humiliated enough.

I've seen Steinberg several times over the years, and our relationship has been friendly. But it's inevitable: any time I dwell too long on that incident, I still find myself getting angry and embittered. It's not the kind of thing you forget.

The bad news is this: regardless of who heads the union, the greatest thing that could happen to NFL salaries would be for the union to go belly up tomorrow. The NFL owners need the NFLPA.

13
ATTENTION NFL PLAYERS: READ THIS CHAPTER

It's no secret: in the NFL, the owners wield the power. They know it, and they throw around their weight accordingly. The question is, why do they get away with it?

According to the critics, including the NFL Players Association, the owners don't care how fairly they conduct their business, how many people they alienate, because they don't really care if their teams win or lose. Win or lose, the 28 NFL teams share revenues. NFL owners, unlike most heads of industry, suffer no financial penalty for their ineptitude. If bank accounts bulge either way, why worry about winning football games?

That's what the critics say. Personally, I've found NFL owners, collectively, to be no more unreasonable, no more self-serving, than any other segment of the industry. There are fools, and there are men of substance, just as there are among players, coaches, and agents.

As for the assertion that NFL owners don't really mind if their teams fail, I don't believe it for a minute.

I can't deny the facts: the millions of dollars paid annually to the NFL by the networks are divided evenly among the 28 teams. Last year each team received about $17.6 million from TV, before it ever lined up for its opening game.

However, don't try to tell me that the owners of Tampa Bay, Green Bay, or any other losing team aren't *trying* to build a winner. Owners are, generally, men with enormous egos. They all lust for the prestige and glamor of a winning football team.

The reason teams lose isn't lack of effort. It's lack of ability. It's not that Robert Irsay wants a winner any less than Al Davis. He just doesn't have the expertise to build one.

I agree with the NFLPA that management, at times, behaves with all the sensitivity of a drunken donkey. But it isn't the owners at fault.

Primarily, I fault the NFLPA.

The owners are running a business, not a charity. And in trying to make a profit, they do whatever they feel is necessary to protect their self-interest. In that respect, why should the owner of a football team be any different from any other employer? As an agent, I expected owners to be difficult, simply because of the nature of our relationship. Hell, I was trying to take money from their pockets.

On the other hand, you would think the NFLPA would have made my job easier. In fact, it was the NFLPA that made my job so tough.

The intransigence of NFL owners had nothing to do with profit sharing. It was like the old joke about why dogs lick their private parts: owners played the heavy because they *could*; they were in a position to.

It was a position the owners secured for themselves from the day they conceived the league. But it was also a position that, in 1977, the NFLPA had a golden opportunity to topple. It was a chance to distribute the power more evenly throughout the industry; to give the players some leverage in their dealings with the owners.

Yet it never happened. The NFLPA, for all its rhetoric about aiding athletes, took that might and handed it right back to the owners. Today, 10 years later, the players are still feeling the financial repercussions. For that, the NFL players can thank Ed Garvey.

Garvey, in 1977, was the NFLPA's executive director. What Garvey inflicted on NFL players was, in my opinion, the biggest sellout by a union in the history of sports. In fact, I think if you chart the entire history of labor and management, you'll have trouble finding a greater betrayer.

I spoke of the overwhelming power held by the NFL owners over their players. Until 1976, that power rested primarily in two mechanisms: the college draft and Rozelle Rule—the compensation rule. These gave the owners tremendous force over the players on two critical fronts: where they worked and for how much profit.

Consider the draft. When an athlete leaves college, there is no bidding among the owners for his services. It doesn't matter if he's lived his whole life in San Diego and wants to stay home and play for the Chargers. If he is drafted by the Cincinnati Bengals, that's where he goes. He isn't like any other American, who can take a job with any company he wants. He isn't like his roommate, the brilliant business student who graduated at the top of his class. Although both are superior to their peers in their abilities, the business student can peddle his services wherever he chooses. The athlete has no such options. If he wants to play in the NFL, he goes to Cincinnati.

The Rozelle Rule was equally restrictive. The rule held that if any player played out his option and joined another NFL team, his former team had to be compensated. The unknown compensation would come in the form of players or draft choices, to be selected by Commissioner Pete Rozelle. The rule functioned as it was intended to: owners, knowing Rozelle would make compensations extremely severe, did not bid on veterans playing out their options. Free agency in the NFL was an illusion.

Together, the draft and the Rozelle Rule kept salaries down, bound players to the teams that drafted them, and made it much more profitable for NFL owners to run their businesses.

In December of 1975, the courts ripped the smiles off the owners' faces. In a case brought by former NFLPA President John Mackey, a U.S. District Court judge declared the Rozelle Rule illegal, in violation of federal antitrust laws. Some players enjoyed the fruits of their liberation as quickly as the following season: John Riggins, Larry Csonka, and Calvin Hill all joined new teams without compensation of their former clubs.

In September of 1976, a U.S. District Court dealt the owners another unprecedented blow. In a suit brought by former Washington Redskin Jim (Yazoo) Smith, the college draft was struck down, also in violation of federal antitrust laws. One month later, the U.S. Appeals Court upheld the decision on the Rozelle Rule. The owners were staggered. For the first time ever, the players and their agents had leverage backed by the courts.

That year I represented Tony Dorsett, Ricky Bell, Marvin Powell, Warren Bryant, and several other college stars. Without the draft, I could sell their services to whoever wanted them most. And on the first day of 1977, I went on national television with Bryant and Dorsett, offering their services to the highest bidder. A few weeks later in the *Washington Post*, I said that any team in the league could win the Super Bowl just by signing the clients I had coming out of college. All they had to do was buck Rozelle.

Rozelle, you see, still believed that the league would get the draft reinstated and he had sent a memo to every team, warning them not to sign any college players. Despite Rozelle's warning, Hugh Culverhouse, Hank Stram, and several other NFL executives showed immediate interest in signing my clients. But none of them followed through; apparently, they chose not to defy the commissioner.

It was clear why Rozelle felt confident that he and the owners would get the draft back. He was hoping the NFLPA would peddle it back to the owners in the upcoming collective bargaining agreement. Under collective bargaining, certain trade practices that would normally be unconstitutional are legal if both the union and management agree to them. I hoped Rozelle was wrong, but having little respect for the union, I feared he could be right. I spoke to the press about my concerns: if the NFLPA returned the draft, I warned, the association's liability would be glaring.

I made no difference. On February 16, 1977, the NFLPA and the NFL owners came to terms on a collective bargaining agreement. The result?

Garvey gave them back the draft.

Garvey gave them back compensation, in an even more restrictive form. Less than one year after it was born, Garvey killed free agency.

What Garvey gained for the players, in comparison to what he lost for them, was a joke. He got a provision for a closed shop: even if a player didn't join the union, he still had to pay the union the annual equivalent of union dues. Garvey got a union dues checkoff: he didn't have to rely on the players themselves to send in their union dues; they were automatically deducted from their paychecks by the teams and sent to the union. For damages arising from *Mackey v. NFL*, the union was awarded $13.65 million, presumably to be paid to 3,200 former and active players over 10 years, payments ranging from less than $200 to $16,500. The union also won concessions on injury grievances as well as several "freedom issues," such as the abolition of rules about hair and dress and the right to have private phones in training camp. Other perfunctory concessions, typical of any collective bargaining agreement, were made.

But the ugly bottom line remains: Garvey traded free

agency and the abolished draft—unprecedented, monumental breakthroughs for the players—for nothing much more than a healthy union treasury.

This presents an obvious question: why would the head of a union sell out his own rank and file?

To me it's always been clear: personal ambition.

Ed Garvey, in some respects, is a genius. And if he used that brilliance in the players' best interests, I'm sure he would have negotiated some superb collective bargaining agreements. But I truly believe that what Garvey held dearest, what mattered more to him ultimately than his constituents, was power, power he couldn't find as head of the NFLPA. So Garvey lusted after bigger game: a career in politics.

No one has ever accused Ed Garvey of lacking an ego. And I believe Garvey, a dyed-in-the-wool Democrat, wanted his fellow party members to perceive him the same way he saw himself: as a blunt-nosed labor leader, defender of solidarity. I also believe that, with the publicity that would come from his clashes with the NFL owners, Garvey saw a pulpit, a steppingstone, from which he could launch a career in politics.

I believe the NFL owners knew this, and they knew Garvey. As collective bargaining approached, they saw he was vulnerable. His union was weak, and funds were low: only 30 percent of the players in the league were dues-paying members. The union, along with its executive director's political aspirations, was in danger of extinction.

So the owners cut a very shrewd deal, one they knew Garvey couldn't resist. They'd get back the draft and eliminate free agency. Their system would once again be legal. In return, Garvey would get his closed shop. The union, financially solvent, would remain afloat. And so would Ed Garvey's ambitions.

I listened to Garvey backers scoff at any suggestion of a sellout. They said Garvey made a prudent move: the union, once staggering, would have the funds to fight the next big collective bargaining battle in 1982. But to my ears, it was hype. Making crucial sacrifices now for potential benefits down the road is one thing if your constituents are auto workers, people who might spend the next 25 years in the same line of work. But in 1977, the average NFL career lasted less than four years. By 1982, a majority of the players wouldn't even be around.

The whole picture Garvey tried to paint of the NFLPA as this gritty labor union was to me a farce in itself. The NFLPA isn't a union in the true sense of the word. It's more like an association or a guild. The true union represents the guy who's working in a coal mine, the woman who's working in a sweatshop, the assembly line worker—the common man who, through collective bargaining, might get a 10 percent raise across the board.

The NFLPA is a different animal. You can't take the ideologies that apply to the normal union and apply them to the NFLPA. The NFLPA isn't working for the rights and privileges of the common working man. It's working for a man with a six-figure income who wants to make a seven-figure income. The members of a normal union believe in gains for all. The players in the NFL are generally still believers in the star system, a system where, through achievement, they can rise to the top. It simply is not the same thing.

There is, however, a quality that the NFLPA shares with many unions: the members are often at the mercy of the union heads, which is precisely what happened to the players. They had no clout whatsoever and little understanding of the issues. The 28 player representatives are the only union members with any real influence. Even if an entire team took an internal vote one way, it didn't bind the player reps to vote accordingly. On the contrary, player reps could, and did, vote any way they wanted. And since all Garvey needed to enact anything was a "yes" vote from 15 player reps (a majority of the total of 28), he essentially controlled the rank and file.

If you're a football fan, 1982 was a year you might rather forget. That was the season of the 57-day players' strike, the longest in the history of sports. Nobody won: the owners lost millions; the players lost roughly 50 percent of their annual salaries; the fans lost nearly half of their season. The strike left the industry reeling.

From what I can determine, about the only thing most insiders agreed upon was on whom to affix the blame: Ed Garvey.

As collective bargaining approached in 1982, Garvey had two big, radical demands: percentage of gross and a centralized method of paying the players. Under Garvey's plan, the players would derive their wages from 55 percent of the NFL teams' total revenues. From that centralized pool of money, every player, regardless of talent or position, would receive the same base salary, depending solely on his tenure in the league.

Garvey said he was simply trying to give the players a larger slice of the pie. Fine, but if that was his only motive, then why did he never once put a demand for free agency back on the bargaining table? Just as he was five years earlier, I believe Garvey was after something bigger. Much bigger.

How so? With salaries based only on tenure, there would no longer be a need for individual negotiations. Agents and owners, removed from the bargaining process, would be nothing more than figureheads. Instead, the game would be dominated by only two men: Garvey, who would negotiate collectively for the players, and Rozelle, who would negotiate collectively for the owners.

Sound absurd? Of course it was. The NFL owners would rather have given Garvey their wives than remove themselves from the salary process.

The players, in return for blindly following Garvey, again got sacrificed. After all the bad blood, the financial loss, the players gained very little. They sure as hell didn't get percentage of gross. To the contrary, I have a copy of the owners' original proposal to the players, which was released to the press *before* the strike. If you put it next to the proposal that Garvey eventually accepted as a collective bargaining agreement, it's almost an exact duplicate.

The union, looking to save some face, pointed to the owners' concession on severance pay. And the players did get higher severance pay, which was obviously a positive thing. But the owners put the severance pay issue on the table *before* the strike. There were minor modifications made afterward, but in no way worthy of a strike.

What I find alarming is that there was barely any negotiation before the strike. The owners made a proposal, the players countered with their own, and then there was a strike. There was a reason for that: Garvey was never a true, hard-grinding negotiator. He was an ideologue.

As events unwound, Garvey's strike made Custer's Last Stand look pretty successful by comparison. It was a waste of energy and money and a blemish on an entire industry. And yet another rout by the owners.

After the strike, there was nowhere for Garvey to go except out of the business. In June of 1983 he retired from the union; as I and others had predicted earlier, he entered politics as assistant attorney general in his native Wisconsin. His career ascended rapidly: last fall, Wisconsin Democrats nominated Garvey to run for United States senator. He was defeated.

Garvey has left the union, but the industry still suffers from the impact of his reign. If not for the collective bargaining agreement validating the draft and compensation, football players would have enjoyed, for the past 10 years, free agency. That would have led to bidding wars and escalating salaries, just as it has in baseball. But football still has no free agency, and look at the result: In 1986, the average salary in baseball was roughly $420,000. In football it was about $225,000. And if the USFL hadn't come along, the comparison would be even more lopsided.

In Garvey's wake, Gene Upshaw is the current head of the union. Much more sympathetic to the needs of the players, Upshaw, a former Raider, is finally seeking free agency. That's the good news.

The bad news is this: regardless of who heads the union, the greatest thing that could happen to NFL salaries would be for the union to go belly up tomorrow. The NFL owners *need* the NFLPA.

Without a union, without a collective bargaining agreement, the owners would be in the same terrifying position they found themselves in briefly during the seventies: they would again be subject to federal antitrust laws. The draft and the Rozelle Rule would again become illegal. NFL salaries would skyrocket.

Unfortunately for the players, it's all conjecture: the union will never go away.

Management won't let it.

The so-called authority of some GMs is laughable. In Philadelphia, Harry Gamble is the GM and VP for Norman Braman. But it always seemed to me that for all his clout, Gamble might as well be Braman's dry cleaner. Braman runs that team from top to bottom.

14
GM WARS

There's a myth about NFL negotiations. They all take place in a smoke-filled room, Cuban cigars blazing, agent versus owner, in a single, grueling, midnight-oil-burning session. The first to blink gets his pocket picked.

It's a kind of romantic image, but that's all it is—an image. I've rarely negotiated a contract in a single meeting. Typically, it's a series of verbal discussions that ultimately results in a formal contract. Often, the guts of the deal get hammered out over the phone.

As for agent pitted against owner, it doesn't work that way. Most negotiations take place with a general manager. But just because the owner isn't physically present, it doesn't mean he's not making all the crucial decisions. With little exception, general managers in the NFL have no real economic power. GMs can cut a player or bring a free agent into camp, but in terms of real economic authority, they have none. They're given a set of numbers by the owner and warned not to exceed it. GMs, no matter how able, mostly take orders. They're lieutenants, not generals.

I recall a negotiation in 1974, when Ron Wolf was doing contracts for the Raiders. Each time we would reach certain salary levels, Wolf would excuse himself to go to the rest room. After several trips, I asked Wolf what he was doing.

"Just between you and me," he said, "I'm going to call Al."

Wolf was calling Al Davis each time we made a jump of five grand or so. Wolf is one of the more knowledgeable men in the game. But that's just the way the NFL works: when an owner buys a team, he wants to exercise the power.

Seniority makes no difference. Johnny Sanders, who'd been GM with the San Diego Chargers for years, couldn't go $1,000 over budget without calling Gene Klein, then the Chargers' owner. During one negotiation, Sanders popped out of the room so many times I finally told him just to let me talk to Klein myself. He did, and Klein and I finished the deal.

The so-called authority of some GMs is laughable. When Edgar Kaiser owned the Denver Broncos, his general manager was Grady Alderman. But Alderman had no influence at all; it was all vested in Kaiser's right-hand man, Hein Poulus. I don't think Alderman could give away a Broncos T-shirt without first getting permission.

In Philadelphia, Harry Gamble is the GM and VP for Norman Braman. But it always seemed to me that for all his clout, Gamble might as well be Braman's dry cleaner. Braman runs that team from top to bottom.

Some GMs are like some owners: they know they hold the cards, so they try to play dictator with you. Or promise you one thing, then have a memory lapse. Neither tactic worked real well with me.

Eddie LeBaron, who once played quarterback for the Dallas Cowboys, had been named GM of the Atlanta Falcons in 1977; I was representing Warren Bryant, the offensive tackle from Kentucky and Atlanta's first pick. LeBaron was coming to Los Angeles on other business. We made a date to discuss Bryant's contract.

It was one of those rarities: we made a deal after a single meeting. We shook hands, and LeBaron left. I was surprised that it had been so painless.

The headaches began a few days later, when I still hadn't received the contracts. I called LeBaron to question the delay. First he gave me some double-talk, then he confessed: the Falcons had had a change of heart; they weren't quite ready to make the deal. They wanted to wait before they did anything final.

I told LeBaron he could wait all he wanted; he wasn't going to talk to me again. There was nothing else for us to discuss. A deal was a deal. And now he'd broken it.

A week later, LeBaron called. He was ready to make another offer for Bryant, he told my secretary. I wouldn't come to the phone. Tell LeBaron, I instructed my secretary, I had only one interest: the original deal, in a formal contract, on my desk. Until then I had nothing to say.

Bryant was a quality prospect, and the people in Atlanta began getting antsy. LeBaron kept calling, but I refused to speak with him. The Atlanta press got in the act: why wouldn't I return LeBaron's phone calls? I told them the same thing I told LeBaron.

Next I got a call from Ron Wolf. He was working for Tampa Bay, and we'd recently done the Ricky Bell deal. I also knew Wolf from his days with the Raiders. Someone with the Falcons, aware that Wolf and I were on good terms, had asked him to call me. As a personal favor to him, Wolf asked me to call LeBaron and resume negotiations. I told Wolf to call me again, anytime, with some other favor. This one I couldn't help him with. LeBaron had broken his word.

As a last resort, Wolf asked if I would at least talk to Curt Mosher, a former employee of Wolf now with Atlanta. I said I'd be happy to.

Mosher and Tom Braatz, Atlanta's director of player personnel, came to Los Angeles, and we met in their suite at the Century Plaza Hotel.

"You've got 15 minutes to make the deal," I told them. "I don't want to waste a lot of time on a contract I've already negotiated."

"Look, I'm going to make this easy," Braatz said. "We're prepared to make the deal we originally agreed upon."

"That's not good enough."

"What do you mean?" Braatz asked.

"Just what I said: it's not good enough. Your first offer is where we'll start. Now I want some punishment money."

"Punishment money? What the hell is that?"

I told him:

I was following a code I had learned when I first entered the business. I heard about it from several executives; Mike Brown, the GM of the Cincinnati Bengals, had explained it to me most explicitly. In the NFL, Brown told me solemnly, you must be a man of your word. Your word is your bond. If you break your word, you will never be a man of respect. And once you've broken that word, even once, you'll be forced to face the consequences: nobody will want to work with you because they'll know you can't be trusted.

I told Braatz I believed in that code. And since LeBaron had broken his word, it was the Falcons who would suffer the consequences. I would work with them, but even if it was just a little bit more, I needed some punishment money. And in future negotiations, if LeBaron ever did the same thing, it would happen again.

Braatz and Mosher gave in. They sweetened the deal by about $25,000, along with some new incentive clauses. Bryant was amazed but delighted when he saw his new contract.

I wasn't bullshitting Braatz: I believed what Brown had told me, and I pride myself on keeping my word. I think a majority of GMs do, too. Throughout my entire career, I had to demand punishment money from only one other GM. It was, of all people, Mike Brown.

In 1980, Anthony Munoz, the All-American tackle from

USC, was drafted by the Bengals. Brown and I hammered out a deal, a six-year pact for $1 million, which included a signing bonus of $250,000. I called Munoz; that night, he and his wife celebrated their good fortune. It had been a difficult negotiation. They were terribly relieved.

About four days later, I still hadn't received the contracts. I called Brown to find out why; I was shocked by his reply.

"The Cincinnati Bengals are not prepared to make this deal," Brown said.

"I don't believe this," I said. "We already made the deal. What happened?"

"I'll say it again. The Cincinnati Bengals are not prepared to make this deal. I don't believe we actually consummated a deal."

"Mike, this has happened to me only one time before, and I'm not going to treat you one bit different than I did Eddie LeBaron. For breaking your word, your own goddamn code, now you're going to have to pay punishment money."

I gave Brown my new price. I vowed Munoz wouldn't sign for 10 cents less.

"Listen, I'm willing to make you an offer right now," Brown said. "It's in the neighborhood of $600,000."

That was $400,000 less than what we'd agreed upon that week. "Save your breath," I told Brown. Then I hung up on him.

For the next three weeks, no word from Brown. I tried a different tactic: I had a lawsuit filed against the Bengals for failure to deal in good faith. I wanted the court to declare Munoz a free agent. My argument was that the NFL draft is a privilege, and when that privilege is abused, it should be revoked.

The Bengals and the NFL appeared in court. Their lawyers asked that the suit be dropped, on the grounds that the court had no jurisdiction; rather, under collective bargaining, there was a procedure for noninjury grievance matters between players and management. And they claimed Munoz's case should be decided not by the courts, but through the grievance apparatus.

We argued that since Munoz was not yet an employee of the NFL, only a prospective one, he shouldn't be bound to the league's procedure. The court ruled in our favor. A hearing date was set for mid-July, to determine whether Munoz would or would not become a free agent.

Suddenly, I started getting calls from Mike Brown.

I wouldn't talk to him. "Tell Brown," I instructed my secretary, "I don't talk to bullshit artists."

After trying my office, unsuccessfully, every day for a week, Brown changed his strategy. He began leaking items to the press about how irate and illogical I was, how I wasn't dealing in good faith, how I was hurting my client more than benefitting him. It had long been part of Brown's style: when putting pressure on an unsigned Bengal, he would try to intimidate him through the press. He even arranged to have the articles mailed to Munoz, with no return address. How do I know it was Brown? He all but admitted it. It made no difference: had we gone to court, we would have proved it ourselves.

That day never came. While I still refused to speak to Brown directly, I did agree to talk with him through a third party, my attorney.

Brown called, and we began to bargain. He raised his six-year offer from $600,000 to $750,000. I said no. He went to $800,000, then $900,000, then $950,000. I still said no. Brown finally went up to $990,000, exactly $10,000 below our original deal. That, he said, was absolutely his final offer. It was transparent: Brown knew he was giving in but felt he could still save face somewhat by refusing me total victory.

Tell Brown, I told my attorney, we'll get back to him. "Let's try this guy on for size," I said. "Let's see how important form is to him over substance."

The Bengals, at the time, had a very strict policy regarding incentive clauses. If a player made the Pro Bowl, he got something like $5,000. If he made All-NFL first team, he got $5,000. That was basically it.

I decided to challenge it. We went back to Brown, said we would concede our $10,000 disagreement, but only if he agreed to certain incentives. If Munoz made All-Rookie, he'd get a bonus of roughly $25,000. If he made the Pro Bowl, and All-NFL, and All-Conference, he'd get $20,000 for each category. These incentive clauses, except for All-Rookie, would hold for each of the six years on Munoz's contract. Brown agreed to all demands.

Although Munoz has had his contract renegotiated since his original deal, those incentive clauses have cost the Bengals in the neighborhood of $200,000. Munoz made his $10,000 back the first year alone, and then some, when he was All-Rookie.

Mike Brown, it was clear, cared more about form than substance. In order to preserve his image, he refused to give in on $10,000 so that the Munoz contract would not read $1 million. Meanwhile, it cost his team about a couple hundred grand.

I had another clash with Brown back in 1976, when I was negotiating for Archie Griffin, the two-time Heisman trophy winner from Ohio State. Brown was even more inflexible in 1976 than he would be later with Munoz. He didn't even believe in negotiating. He felt agents were intrusive and unnecessary. The Bengals would draft a player; Brown would insist on making him an offer to his face and refuse to deal on that offer. That was his idea of negotiating.

I wanted a six-figure signing bonus for Archie, but I had a pretty strong feeling I wouldn't get it. The Bengals had a policy of not giving out six-figure signing bonuses to anyone. So before I went to Brown, I devised a plan to fall back on. Shortly after the Bengals drafted Archie, I had enlisted an offer from the Montreal Alouettes of the CFL. It was a poor offer, much less than we were asking. Brown, of course, didn't know this. I took the CFL offer and stuck it in my briefcase. Then, with Archie and his brother Jim, I went to see Brown.

Brown offered a $45,000 signing bonus. I told him, no, we wanted six figures, or we weren't going to sign. I also told him we'd been approached by the Montreal Alouettes; if Brown refused to be more reasonable, we'd have to consider going there.

Brown was characteristically arrogant. He implied that this deal would be a hell of a lot easier without the interference of an agent. "We want Archie Griffin, he wants us, there's no reason to discuss this any further. I've made you a good offer, it's our final offer, and I suggest you take it."

I pulled out the contracts from the Alouettes. "Archie, sign these contracts." Archie, as I'd instructed him before the meeting, signed the contracts. Then I turned back to Brown. "Listen, Mike, you're not dealing with Archie Griffin now. You're dealing with Mike Trope. These are contracts from the Montreal Alouettes. And the distance between Archie and Montreal is the distance between myself and the mailbox. They're signed. I mail them, he's their property. You're history."

Brown wasn't exactly impressed. "Do I think you're being silly? Yes, I do. Do I think you're bluffing? Yes, I do. Am I going to move off my offer? No, I'm not."

Just like that, he'd shot us down. The three of us stood to leave. As we headed for the door, we were waiting for that last-minute plea. It never came. We walked out to silence.

We drove to the airport, the whole way cursing Brown for being such an obstinate son-of-a-bitch. We were approaching the ticket counter when I heard a page over the airport intercom. It was Brown. He wanted us to come back.

We returned to Brown's office and got what we wanted: a

signing bonus of $100,000, along with a few more kickers, bringing the bonus to about $125,000. It was the first time in history that the Bengals had given a rookie a six-figure bonus to sign. After it was over, Brown was acting like he was glad to do it. "Well, if I'm going to give anyone a six-figure bonus, I might as well give it to a quality person like Archie Griffin."

Brown pulled me to the side a few minutes later. He asked if I'd been serious about taking Archie to the CFL. I told him I was. That I hadn't was none of his business.

Mike Brown, perhaps more than any GM in the league, has a reputation as a tough negotiator. In truth, Brown isn't a negotiator at all. He's part of an old school of NFL management, who, for the majority of their careers, never had to truly negotiate. With a draft, no free agency, and total inflexibility of movement by the players, Brown doesn't have to negotiate. He can just sit back, decide what he wants to pay, and wait. The only time Brown negotiates is when he has to: when an agent has leverage, such as the USFL, or such as I did with Munoz or Griffin. The only thing that got those players more money was leverage. Not the generosity of Mike Brown's heart.

I consider Brown the most unreasonable person I ever dealt with in the NFL. And, when it came to negotiating contracts, also the most arrogant. That's why I never hesitated to exploit whatever leverage I had. You couldn't feel sorry for a guy like Brown. When the tables were turned, he wouldn't feel sorry for you.

I once read a quote from Dan Rooney, owner of the Steelers: "There's no correlation between how aggressively people play and how they negotiate."

It's true. There's also no correlation between how aggressively management *wants* people to play and how it *wants* them to negotiate. On the field, management wants players who are fearless, cunning, warlike. At contract time, they'd like the exact same player to be afraid of his shadow. Hopefully, his agent will be the same way.

At contract time, I've heard it all. I've had management attack my client's intelligence: "Well, we gave him an IQ test, and he's not too smart. It'll take him longer to learn our system." His anatomy: "He's got a bad back. We took a chance on him." His physical ability: "He's slow, and he has no hands. He's a good backup receiver. But that's it." When the player was drafted, he was Staubach and Payton rolled into one. When it came to paying him, he was Bozo the Clown.

GMs yank out one player's contract to whittle down his teammate's deal. In other words: "Hey, so and so only got this, so your guy isn't about to get any more than that." One time I gave Mike Brown a dose of this particular medicine. And Brown splashed it back in my face.

It was during the Archie Griffin negotiations. I had just signed Chuck Muncie to a $200,000 signing bonus, which at the time was revolutionary. While negotiating for Archie, I pulled out Muncie's contract with New Orleans and showed it to Brown. Brown glanced, said nothing, and walked to his file cabinet. He pulled out a contract.

"Let me show you how relevant I consider Muncie's contract to what we're doing with the Bengals," Brown said.

Brown showed me a player's contract from the 1950s. A first-round pick, he'd gotten a signing bonus of $500. His salary for the entire year had been $5,000.

"Okay, you got a $200,000 signing bonus for Muncie," Brown said. "Well, we got this guy for five hundred bucks. This guy's contract isn't relevant to you, so why should Muncie's contract be relevant to us? We're smart here; that's what separates us from the rest of the league. You want a sucker? Go back to New Orleans."

When a GM does get leveraged into giving a player a substantial contract, even if it is perfectly fair, some find it difficult to admit it. It's an ego thing: they don't want to look weak, compromised, in the eyes of the other GMs.

Mike Lynn, general manager for the Minnesota Vikings, is a good example of this, though he's hardly the only one. Lynn enjoys his reputation for being notoriously stingy. And rather than concede that he'd given a player an adequate contract, Lynn would disguise the actual numbers; he'd make the contract appear much smaller than it really was. Lynn could then go to league meetings and brag about how cheaply he'd signed his players: "Hell, I gave my first-round pick only eighty grand. You gave yours a hundred." This accomplished two things: It made Lynn feel, in front of his peers, like he was a real ballbreaker. It also had a ripple effect, downward, on salaries across the league. When one GM hears another is toeing the bottom line, he's encouraged to try the same thing.

Lynn used a simple yet effective measure to disguise the true numbers. He would "hide" extra cash on the back of the players' contracts.

An NFL contract, unless it has an unusual number of added provisions, consists of only one page. On the front of that page is a space for a player's yearly base salary, his bread and butter, so to speak. When industry people discuss a player's salary, they usually refer only to the base.

Backside provisions are just that: they're added in, on the back of that one page. Backside provisions normally include what we call "honor" clauses; for instance, bonuses for making All-Pro or gaining 1,000 yards. If the clauses are realized, they're great. But since there are so many intangibles involved—health, good blocking, whatever—no one really banks on honor clauses. So, like fine print, no one pays much attention to the backside.

What Lynn (and other GMs) will do is take a contract's backside and stick in *substantial* provisions. They'll actually say to an agent, "Look, I'll give you another $20,000; but only if we put it in back." It might be worded on the contract as a $20,000 bonus, rather than a $20,000 guarantee. But it's a bonus for something your grandmother could accomplish, like reporting two days early to camp. Then, speaking only of the base, a GM can tell everybody he got off $20,000 easier than he actually did.

A few years ago I represented Steve Bono, the UCLA quarterback, whom the Vikings made their sixth-round pick. Lynn came into Los Angeles and showed me that he'd recently signed another Viking six-rounder for a $10,000 signing bonus and a one-year deal for $55,000. He offered me the same numbers for Bono. I gave Lynn a hard-line no. When training camp approached, still without progress, Lynn started to get nervous.

Lynn then made an offer that I accepted. On the surface, it appeared that Bono got a $10,000 signing bonus, a $5,000 roster bonus, and a $55,000 salary for one year. It seemed at a glance that Lynn had won the war: with the exception of the $5,000, it looked as if I had relented to his original offer. Lynn liked that.

The whole thing was fine with me, too: the extra cash was hidden on the backside.

Cosmetically, the only money guaranteed to Bono was the $10,000 signing bonus. Here was the real deal:

The $55,000 base, the $10,000 signing bonus, and the $5,000 roster bonus were all deferred until six months into the following year. The Vikings gave Bono a $75,000 loan, which didn't have to be repaid until the following year, when he'd already gotten all his deferred money. Most important, there was a provision in the promissory note: if Bono didn't make the team, he would not have to repay the loan. Which meant Bono was guaranteed $75,000, not $10,000. The average rookie guarantee that year was about $33,000. The Vikings gave Bono twice that.

Also, the Vikings signed Bono to the standard one-year option they offered all rookies: if his option was picked up, he'd get a 10 percent increase on his original salary. However, and this was on the backside, he'd also receive an additional bonus of $20,000 when the club exercised the option, and the increase in salary for the option year wasn't 10 percent, but something like 89 percent. Bottom line: What looked like a two-year deal (if Bono's option was picked up) for roughly $130,000 was really a two-year deal for approximately $210,000. What looked like a $10,000 guarantee in the form of a rookie signing bonus was really a $75,000 guarantee.

Despite the fact that he remained on the bench for two years and was finally waived, Bono, a sixth-round pick with ordinary college statistics, had done pretty well for himself. Despite, I'm sure, what Lynn told his buddies at the NFL meetings.

Irsay took a deep slug from his drink. Then he pulled a wad of hundred-dollar bills from his pants pocket and began to count them. "One, two, three, four. Come on, Mike. Come on, come on, come on. How much do you want to make a deal? Come on, come on!"

15
THE OWNERS: BOYS AND THEIR TOYS

Robert Irsay, owner of what was then the Baltimore Colts, moved his franchise to Indianapolis in 1984. Though heartbroken, Colts fans should not have been totally surprised. Privately and in public, Irsay had threatened to leave the city many times.

"One day I'm just going to get the moving vans and leave," Irsay would storm around his office and tell his employees.

And as we all know, that's just what Irsay did. But he did it under the cover of darkness, vans leaving the city in the middle of the night. It was brazen, bizarre, illogical. In short, it was Robert Irsay.

I've dealt with Irsay myself. On my list of strange encounters with NFL owners, I'd rank the one I had with Irsay squarely at the top.

In 1981 I represented Johnie Cooks, a rookie linebacker from Mississippi State, in his contract negotiations with the

Colts. I was contacted by Mike Chernoff, the Colts' vice president and attorney in charge of negotiations. Chernoff said he'd be coming into the Los Angeles airport; I should meet him at the airport bar to discuss Cooks's contract.

For 90 minutes at the bar, we bargained, never closed a deal, but did at least break some ground. Chernoff then suggested I speak with Irsay myself. Irsay was also at the airport, he said, at the airstrip that catered only to private planes. If I was agreeable, Irsay would meet me on his Learjet. I said that was fine.

When I entered the jet, I was greeted by Irsay, who was standing in the aisle, one hand wrapped around a cocktail glass, the other clutching the top of a seat. Face flushed and grinning, he appeared to be smashed. When his breath hit me like the heat from an oven, I had a pretty good clue that he was.

Considering we were about to negotiate a contract, I wasn't pleased that Irsay had been drinking. But it also wasn't unexpected. Irsay's fondness for a beverage had been a public issue in Baltimore for years. Bert Jones once told the *Baltimore Sun* that Irsay was "a liar, a cheat, crude, with no manners, and he drinks too much." Irsay's drinking was certainly no secret among his peers. I'd been told by several NFL owners that he would sometimes show up drunk at league meetings.

Now, in midafternoon, Irsay seemed more lit up than the Orange Bowl. When he spoke—try to imagine this—he sounded like a drunken Walter Brennan.

"Hey, Mike!" Irsay yelled. "How the hell you doing? Chernoff, did you and Mike sign up our boy?"

"No, Mr. Irsay," Chernoff said. "We're still a way off on this one."

Irsay pouted at me. "What's the problem, Mike? Why can't we make a deal right now?"

I told Irsay it was money. He asked me to outline our demands, which I did. Irsay looked cheered.

"That sounds reasonable to me," Irsay said. "Hell, you got a deal! Let's shake on it."

I glanced at Chernoff; he looked like he'd eaten some rotten fruit for breakfast. But Irsay still offered his hand, so I went to shake it. When our hands were an inch apart, Irsay yanked his back. "Only kidding, only kidding," Irsay chortled. "I never shook your hand, so it ain't no deal."

Irsay turned to the pilot, who'd been watching our exchange. "You never saw me shake, did you?" Irsay said. "Did you ever see me shake his hand?"

"No, sir, I didn't," said the pilot.

"It's a good thing you said that," Irsay said quickly. "If you hadn't, I'd have *fired* you, you son-of-a-bitch."

Irsay turned to Chernoff. "Chernoff, did you ever see me shake his hand?"

"No, Mr. Irsay, I never saw you shake his hand," Chernoff said.

"Good," Irsay said. "Because if you said I had, I'd have fired you, *too*, you son-of-a-bitch."

Irsay offered me a drink; I said, sure, I'd take a Coke. Irsay walked to the bar, brought back my glass, and gave it to me. I took a sip and nearly spit it back on my lap. It tasted like lighter fluid. It was Coke, all right, mixed with about three-quarters rum. Irsay was laughing so hard I thought he might pee.

"Goddamnit," I screamed, "you spiked my drink!"

"What the hell do you mean?" Irsay said. "That's Coca-Cola. Chernoff, come over here and taste this man's drink."

Poor Chernoff. He walked over, cleared his throat, and took a small sip.

"That's Coke all right, boss," he said, eyes watering.

"Good," Irsay said. "Because if you said it wasn't, I'd have *fired* you, you son-of-a-bitch."

Irsay gave the taste test to the pilot. The pilot screwed up his face and said it tasted like Coke to him. Irsay told him it was a good thing he said that. Otherwise, he'd have to fire the son-of-a-bitch.

Irsay told the pilot to start the plane and take it up to 25,000 feet. "Take our friend Mike up there. Maybe then he'll make a deal."

Before he could return to the cockpit, Irsay told the pilot he was "only kidding, only kidding."

I felt sorry for Chernoff and the pilot; had they contradicted him, I seriously believe Irsay might have fired them on the spot. Irsay, on the other hand, was beginning to make my teeth grind.

I was contemplating what to do next, when Irsay pinched me, hard, on the cheek, like I was the little kid and he was the uncle. "Come on now, Mike, you and I can make a deal."

He took a deep slug from his drink. Then he pulled a wad of hundred-dollar bills from his pants pocket and began to count them. "One, two, three, four. Come on, Mike. Come on, come on, come on. How much do you want to make a deal? Come on, come on!"

At that point, it was difficult to tell if Irsay was kidding, or simply smashed, or what. But ostensibly, he was trying to buy me off. He wanted to slide me some money on the side; in exchange, I'd lower my demands for my client. I played along with him.

"Look," I said, "you'd have to put up enough money to give Cooks what he wants, and some profit on top of that for me. You want to talk that kind of money, we can talk as long as you want."

Irsay, suddenly gloomy, jutted out his lower lip. "You know something, Mike? You're no fun."

Irsay stood up and said he had to go to the bathroom. It was now or never. I promised Chernoff I'd call him and close the deal. Then I just about ran him over getting off the plane.

Owners buy into football teams with various motivations. I know of one who was almost like a groupie. He seemed to get some perverse gratification out of associating with athletes. That the athletes didn't necessarily want to hang out with him was immaterial. He was the boss.

This guy got his big chance when several businessmen were looking for investors for their franchise; the president and principal owner didn't have the bankroll for the operation, and there was still a great need for capital. Then the aforementioned gentleman came along, with about 90 percent of the investment. For his 90 percent investment, he was offered only 20 percent of the team. He accepted and became a minority owner.

Before too long, however, the team had a money crunch, and the principal owner went to him for additional help; could he begin paying the coaches and players? He agreed to pick up more of the bills, and he insisted on paying the players personally. He'd have the players and coaches drive over to his company to get their paychecks in person. He'd issue checks with his name on them so that the players knew for a fact they were getting paid by him.

He was a walking billboard for his team. He had watches, jackets, decals on his car. At one point, he started going to games with pockets full of cash. Right before the game, he'd offer on-the-spot incentive clauses. If a player had so many sacks, so many yards, so many touchdowns, he'd get a cash bonus immediately following the game, straight from the owner's pockets.

I recall one player who was admiring this guy's watch before a game. He told the player if he gained 100 yards the watch was his. The player came up about 20 yards short. In the parking lot after the game, the owner took off his watch and stuck it under the tire of the team bus.

After one big victory, he truly outdid himself, which was no minor accomplishment. It was in 1975, and I was in the locker room with a client who played on the team. The players were going about their business, stripping off their pads and heading for the showers. Suddenly the owner burst in. He was in ecstasy, jumping up and down, screaming like a cheerleader, as if they'd just won the goddamn Super Bowl. He ran up to one of the players, just about threw himself into his arms, and started yelling: "We won! We won! We won!" The player smiled weakly and continued getting undressed.

He was undaunted. Still beaming, he looked around at his players . . . and decided he would take a shower too! He scrambled out of his clothes and rushed into the shower with his players. As I said good-bye to my client, I could still hear him in the shower with his players, screaming.

I say this with all due love and affection: no one in the NFL can keep his mouth shut. Football people are like anyone else: they love a little gossip.

16
KEEPING SECRETS

I've never had a fistfight with a GM or an owner. Once, however, I nearly ran over an assistant GM with my car.

It started over a secret that wasn't really a secret.

In June of 1980, Johnnie Johnson, a rookie cornerback from the University of Texas, became the highest-paid player on the Rams. I got Johnnie a six-year deal for just over $1 million, with nothing deferred. It had been a pleasant negotiation. I had handed GM Don Klosterman my proposal for Johnnie's contract, left, and the next morning he had called me back to accept. It was one of the simplest negotiations I'd ever conducted. The problems began later, when Johnnie's teammates found out what he was getting.

Until the Rams' owner Carroll Rosenbloom's death the year before, all-cash contracts like Johnnie's had been unprecedented for the Rams. All the Rams' top veterans—Dennis Harrah, Vince Ferragamo, Jack and Jim Youngblood, to name a few—had their payments stretched out over several years. Some hadn't wanted deferred deals, but that was what Rosenbloom gave them anyway. Along comes Johnnie: he's not just getting *all* cash; he's getting *more* cash.

The day after Johnnie signed, the figures were in the morning papers. The veterans revolted; several of the team's top stars refused to report to camp. The Rams front office was outraged—not that they'd made the deal, of course, but that now all the veterans knew about it.

The climate surrounding salaries was different in 1980 than it is today, or even than it was when the USFL or old AFL was around. Today the NFLPA discloses all salaries. When the USFL or AFL were around, the upstart leagues would sign players and brag about how much they were paying them, just to show the NFL and the public how uptown they were.

In 1980, management was skittish about revealing certain salaries, especially the higher ones, because it didn't want one player to know what his teammates were making. If he did, you might have a situation like the one they had with the Rams.

It's not as if the players wouldn't discuss their contracts with each other. There was always talk in the locker room, but you never knew what was real and what was fiction. A disgruntled player might tell everyone he was making $10,000 less than what he was really making and not even mention his signing bonus. Or you might have a braggart who'd pump his salary up. It was hard to determine the bottom line.

Anyway, when Johnnie's contract went public, the Rams front office, looking for a culprit, blamed me. They insisted that I had leaked the numbers to the press.

They were wrong.

I never told Johnnie's figures to anybody. Johnnie got a call the night after he signed from a reporter for the *Los Angeles Times*. He asked Johnnie for the details. Johnnie said he couldn't disclose them, but he did say that he considered "Mrs. [Georgia] Rosenbloom to be like Mrs. Santa Claus to me and my family." Then the same reporter called me. I told him I couldn't give him the particulars, but that Johnnie was now one of the highest-paid defensive backs in the league. I thought I was on safe ground. I had verbally agreed with the Rams' GM, Don Klosterman, not to give out details, and I hadn't. Neither had Johnnie.

The Rams thought I was full of shit.

There was much bad blood, mostly between me and Klosterman. I was angry for two reasons: I was getting blamed for something I hadn't done; and the Rams knew, full well, the press could have discovered Johnnie's deal from a hundred different places.

How so?

I say this with all due love and affection: no one in the NFL can keep his mouth shut. Football people are like anyone else: they love a little gossip.

Let's say the Bears sign a player. Later that day their GM gets a call from the Browns' GM. "Let me know what you got him for," says the Browns' GM. "I won't tell anyone." They're pals, so the guy from the Bears tells the guy from the Browns. The next day the GM from the Steelers calls his GM buddy from the Browns. Word spreads again. By the end of the week, the whole goddamn league knows. It's even worse when a GM knows he's pulled a fast one, signed a guy for peanuts. He can't call his buddies fast enough.

I'm not saying I was exempt. I wasn't. For instance, I'd sign a top pick with one team, then I'd get a call from a GM from another team. He'd say, "Mike, tell me what you got. I've got my own guys to sign. I don't want to give them too much or too little." If it was a GM I had no regard for, I'd tell him I couldn't disclose it. But if it was a GM I was friendly with, I'd tell him what I got. It was partly friendship, partly good business. I've done him a favor; now he owes me one.

Before I get back to the Rams, though, I've got a story that illustrates perfectly just how "sacred" those secrets really are in the NFL.

I had just finished negotiating a player's contract, when I received a call from Harold Guiver, the GM of the Saints. He wanted to know what I got, but his reputation preceded him. He was the Rona Barrett of NFL GMs.

"I'm not going to tell you, Harold," I said. "I've got a confidentiality agreement with the team. Also, I think you've got a big mouth."

"Mike, I swear to God I won't tell anyone. I just need to know because I'm signing players."

I wanted to see for myself if Guiver could keep his word. So I wrote out some numbers on a piece of paper. Except they weren't the real numbers. They were very close, but I made some slight changes. For instance, if my client got a $200,000 signing bonus, I wrote down $206,000. If he got $150,000 a year, I wrote $159,000. When I was done, I read the bogus figures to Guiver. He thanked me and swore again to keep quiet.

Less than two hours later, I got a call from another GM. He started laughing. "Guess what?" he said. "I think I know what you got for your man. He was enjoying himself. GMs love to impress you with how much access they have to everyone else's numbers.

"Baloney," I said. "You don't know what I got him."

I told him to give me the figures he had. They were precisely the numbers—the wrong ones—I had given Guiver. I asked the GM who his source was. He said he had a friend in the league office, a secretary, who had passed them along. I told him that was bullshit and hung up. Then I called Guiver.

"Goddamn it, Harold," I screamed, "you're just like a little old lady. Can't you keep your goddamn mouth shut? The day isn't even over, and already you broke your word to me."

Guiver was stunned. "Jesus, Mike, I swear I didn't tell anyone."

I told him *that* was bullshit. Then I told him the name of the GM I'd just spoken to. Guiver put me on hold: I'm sure he was calling the guy on the other line. Guiver got back on the line and repeated that, no, he hadn't told anyone. The reason he did that, I'm equally sure, was that the other GM had assured him that he hadn't implicated him.

I finally told Guiver what I had done. "Look, Harold, you got caught with your hand in the cookie jar. I gave you erroneous numbers, and you gave them to the first GM who called."

The point of the story, to get back to the Rams, is that the guy from the *Times* could have found out about Johnnie's contract from anyone. And whoever gave it to the *Times* could very well have gotten the numbers from the Rams. I mean, there's no way the Rams didn't tell *someone* what Johnnie got. They blamed me for one reason: the players were angry at them, so they needed a scapegoat to deflect the heat onto. When in doubt, indict the agent.

Three months after Johnnie signed, I had some business at Rams Park, where the Rams hold practice. I went there with my friend Ernie Wright, the former lineman for the San Diego Chargers. We were talking to one of the Rams when Klosterman drove up in his golf cart. The last time I'd seen Don in person, he'd been all smiles.

That was before the veterans' walkout. Now, Klosterman literally wouldn't even look at me.

"I'll talk to you," he said icily to Ernie, "but I won't talk to him. I don't even want him here."

The hell with Rams Park; I could do my business over the phone. I started back to the Rams parking lot to get my car, when I saw Jack Faulkner, the Rams' assistant GM, hurrying toward me. Faulkner is a former pro football player, big and rough-looking; if he was an actor, you'd cast him as a guy named Rocco.

But Faulkner was friendly. Smiling, he said Klosterman had sent him to kick me off the premises, so that's what he was doing. As we were standing there chatting, Pat Thomas walked up. Thomas was a starting cornerback, one of several Rams disgruntled over his contract. Thomas asked me if I was Mike Trope. When I said I was, he asked me for my phone number. Suddenly, Faulkner turned hostile.

"Not on company time," he said. "You won't solicit players here."

"I'm not soliciting," I said. "He asked *me* for my number."

Faulkner, six feet, 250 pounds, called me a dirty name. Don't ask me why, but I, 5'10", 190, called him one back. Bad move. Faulkner shoved me up against my car, then clamped his left hand around my throat. He pulled back his other fist like he was about to smash my face in.

Thank God for Ernie Wright.

When Faulkner drew back his fist, Ernie jumped on his back and wrapped him in a bear hug. While Ernie held Faulkner, I got in my car and started it up. I may be dumb, but I'm not stupid. Fighting Faulkner would have been suicidal.

As I was slowly pulling away in my car, I checked my rearview mirror to see what was happening. I couldn't believe it. Faulkner had broken away and was chasing me. And he was catching up.

That wouldn't do. I slammed on the brakes, yanked on the stick, and stuck the car in reverse. I started backing up, rapidly, in Faulkner's direction.

When he saw me coming right at him, Faulkner's eyes got big. Suddenly, he stopped and began to run the other way. I chased him in reverse for a couple of yards. Then I stopped, picked up Ernie, and drove away.

Several local writers had seen the whole thing. Naturally, there were stories in the papers the following morning. The one in the *Times* was the best. Semiserious, it printed both of our pictures, beside a "Tale of the Tape." It listed our height, weight, age, etc. Under "reach" for Faulkner, it said *Boardinghouse*. For his fist it said *Dangerous*.

I wound up suing Faulkner and the Rams for assault and battery. The Rams hired an attorney to take my deposition. I was familiar with him, he was a fine attorney, but in the course of my deposition he began making innuendos to the effect that he'd heard rumors that I dealt drugs. When I lashed back, it started getting ugly.

This attorney had a habit of leaning way back in his chair so it could balance on only two legs. Right in the midst of a bitter exchange, he tipped so far back that his chair flipped completely over. He went over with it, crashing hard on the tile floor.

The room was silent. I swear, he looked like he was dead. For 30 seconds, he just lay there on the floor, motionless. He finally started coughing; he'd only had the wind knocked out of him.

I glanced at Faulkner, and he seemed to be thinking the same thing I was: "What the hell are we doing here? A guy almost got killed over this bullshit?"

We finished the deposition after a short recess. Eventually, though, I dropped the suit and made amends with Faulkner. Klosterman, too. To this day, I'm friends with both of them.

"Mike, what we need is a plan, a scheme. Something to convince the Oilers they've got damaged goods, that they don't really want Earl. Crippling migraine headaches. Or some mysterious disease. They'd want to get rid of Earl."

—Carroll Rosenbloom,
trying to get Earl Campbell
to play for the Rams.

17
A SUITCASE FULL OF CASH

Carroll Rosenbloom was on the phone. His mood was anything but bright.

It was late January 1979. A few days earlier, the Pittsburgh Steelers had beaten the Dallas Cowboys in Super Bowl XIII. Rosenbloom, owner of the Los Angeles Rams, was still agonizing: had the Rams beaten Dallas in the NFC championship, they, not the Cowboys, would have gone to the Super Bowl.

"There was only one goddamn thing that kept me out of the Super Bowl," Rosenbloom said.

I asked him what that was.

"Earl-fucking-Campbell."

"I was supposed to have him on my team in the first place," he went on. "If I had had him this year, we could have gone right to the Super Bowl. And we would have won the goddamn thing. The kid's amazing."

Rosenbloom paused and lowered his voice. "Uh, by the way, is Earl going to be out in Los Angeles for the Pro Bowl?"

207

The Pro Bowl was the week after the Super Bowl. Earl, who'd just completed his rookie season with the Houston Oilers, would be there.

"Can you do me a little favor, Mike?"

"What's that, Mr. Rosenbloom?"

"When Earl gets out here, let's set a lunch date for the three of us. Let's keep it a secret, all right, Mike? Nothing formal, just a little chat."

I told Rosenbloom we'd try to make it.

I didn't know Rosenbloom well, but I liked him. He seemed a rainbow of contradictions, equal parts warm and combative, charming and spiteful, brutally direct and an expert at manipulation. In his clashes with the other owners, Rosenbloom appeared to love the battle as much as the outcome: he would determine what he wanted, then devise the most exciting, ingenious way to get it.

That the Rams had never been to a Super Bowl was one of the great frustrations of Rosenbloom's life. He felt his team lacked only one ingredient: a dynamic runner. Earl, a brilliant, punishing fullback, fit the bill precisely.

Rosenbloom had already tried for Earl once, when he came out of Texas the year before as the Heisman trophy winner. Tampa Bay, picking first in the draft, had seemed ripe for a trade: the team already had Ricky Bell in its backfield. Rosenbloom sent his general manager, Don Klosterman, to Tampa Bay to wine and dine their front office. In the interim, I received several optimistic calls from Rosenbloom. Klosterman, he was sure, could pull it off.

Able as he was, Klosterman couldn't. Tampa Bay made a deal, but not with the Rams. They traded their pick to Houston, and the Oilers subsequently drafted Earl. The week of the trade, I got a call from Rosenbloom. He was screaming bloody murder. He'd been certain Earl was his, and now he'd lost him.

Rosenbloom's mood didn't improve after Earl's rookie

season. Earl won Rookie of the Year and led the league in rushing. Houston, which had finished only 8-6 the season before, won two playoff games and went all the way to the AFC Championship. The Rams meanwhile fell one win short of the Super Bowl.

Now Rosenbloom was inviting Earl and me to his home.

A few days before the Pro Bowl, I picked up Earl and drove to Rosenbloom's mansion. He lived in the most exclusive part of Bel Air, an old, verdant Los Angeles community noted for its wealth. Rosenbloom took us on a tour of his spectacular home, including the guest bedroom where, Rosenbloom noted, Teddy Kennedy used to sleep on his trips to Los Angeles. Over lunch prepared by his personal Chinese chef, Rosenbloom made clear the intent of our meeting.

"Look, Earl, you know I want you on the Rams," he said. "And if I can get you on my team, I will substantially increase your contract. If I have to double it, that's what I'll do. I want you out here in California."

I reminded Rosenbloom what he already knew: Earl had signed a seven-year deal with Houston. He still had six years left.

Rosenbloom shrugged. "Now Mike, you know I'd be happy to give the Oilers fair compensation in a trade for Earl. But you also know the Oilers are not going to trade a player like Earl under ordinary circumstances."

Rosenbloom continued, his eyes now getting excited. "Mike, what we need is a plan, a scheme. Something to convince the Oilers they've got damaged goods, that they don't really want Earl. Some sort of problem that there's no true way to verify, where all they know is what the patient is telling them. Crippling migraine headaches. Or some mysterious disease. Whatever it is, it has to be something serious. If the Oilers thought nobody else knew about it, and suddenly the Rams came along offering a trade, they would think they had their suckers. They'd *want* to get rid of Earl. If we can set that kind of scenario, I think we can make this work."

Nobody spoke for a moment. Earl asked Rosenbloom if he minded if he checked out the billiards room. When Earl left the room, Rosenbloom put the final glitter on his offer.

"Mike, I know you've got a Machiavellian mind, and I'm counting on you to think of something good. If you can work it out, I'll give you a suitcase with a quarter of a million dollars. Cash."

Rosenbloom stared at me, waiting for my reaction. Early in my career, who knows, I might have been shocked. But by 1979, I'd been in the business for seven years. *Nothing* could amaze me at that point.

Rosenbloom's scheme was crazy, impossible. I just laughed.

There was another reason I wasn't astonished by Rosenbloom's offer, or by anything else the other 27 NFL owners did. My background gave me a certain attitude toward wealth. A lot of people have a preconceived notion about those with great wealth: they think they're almost immortal—or, at the least, very, very special. I've never had that illusion. I grew up around money. And I can tell you, unequivocally, that it does not make men extraordinary. A rich man can still be a drunk, he can still be a lunatic, he can still be a con artist. Knowing that, I never allowed myself to be intimidated or patronized or bullied, just because a rich man owned a football team. I adopted that attitude from the onset of my career. In terms of my relationship with owners, it was one of the primary factors in the measure of my success.

Our meeting with Rosenbloom broke up shortly after he made his offer. I didn't want to dull his interest in Earl, so I simply told him I would explore the situation with Houston and get back to him. Of course, we never tried Rosenbloom's scam. That's not to say I forgot about it; while Earl was content with the Oilers, he also liked

Rosenbloom and found the thought of playing for the Rams appealing. We decided to shake up the Oilers, our own way, and see what happened.

If Earl was so valuable to the Rams—Rosenbloom had promised to double his contract—I figured the Oilers should feel the same way. A few months later, I wrote to the Oilers, demanding a renegotiation. I said we wanted much bigger money, including a $1 million signing bonus. I knew the Oilers wouldn't meet our price, but I was hoping they'd at least give Earl a raise. If they became enraged and refused to renegotiate, we could demand a trade, and Rosenbloom would be there in a minute. I really didn't see that happening, though; I saw a renegotiation as much more likely than a trade.

As I waited for the Oilers' reply, Klosterman, then Rosenbloom, called to check on any progress. I told them I'd keep them posted.

While we were waiting, Rosenbloom died.

He drowned on April 2, 1979, two months after our meeting, near his home off the coast of Florida. In his 70s, he apparently went for a swim on a cool, windy day when the Atlantic was treacherous. His body, lifeless, was found later that day.

Earl Campbell wound up staying with the Houston Oilers, who tore up his contract and gave him a better one. He retired from pro football in 1986.

There was another reason I reacted so calmly to Rosenbloom's unusual proposal to acquire Earl Campbell. I'd gotten a dose of his style a few seasons earlier.

Rosenbloom called me in May 1977, the week after the NFL draft. My office was frenzied: it was the year I represented four of the first five draft choices, including Ricky Bell and Tony Dorsett. In Tony's case, things had started moving before the draft. The Heisman trophy winner from Pitt, Tony was on the verge of getting drafted by the Seattle Seahawks. The problem was he didn't want to go there.

(A word about Tony Dorsett: he's had some difficult times off the field—a divorce, periodic spats with management, the outburst when the Cowboys signed Herschel Walker— and over the years, the Dallas press has had a field day. From my own experience, Tony's a much better person than he's been portrayed. He can be stubborn, and sometimes he speaks before he thinks. So what—he's human. On balance, he's a good man.)

Though it's rare, sometimes an agent can manipulate events behind the scenes to try to dissuade a team from drafting his client. I happened to pull it off in Tony's case, but right up to the day of the draft, it didn't look good. Most people outside the league don't know it, but Tony's cele- brated career as a Cowboy almost never happened. Had circumstances been just a little different, today he might be a Seattle Seahawk.

It was Seattle, not Dallas, that originally had the second pick in the draft, and the Seahawks made it clear they planned on taking Tony. Tony was distraught. He wanted to play for a contender; the Seahawks, in their first season in the league the year before, had gone 2-12. Further, Seattle was a nice enough city, but endorsement possibilities would be minimal. Tony asked me to somehow change the Sea- hawks' intentions.

I took the blunt route: I drafted a letter, notifying the Seahawks that Tony had no desire to play there, so please do not pick him in the upcoming draft. I had no idea how the Seahawks would react. If they wanted Tony badly enough, they could tell us to go to hell, draft him, and see where the cards fell.

But we had some leverage: the Canadian Football League. In the past, when I couldn't come to terms with the NFL, I had taken Johnny Rodgers and Anthony Davis to play in the CFL. I told the Seahawks I could always take

Tony there, too. It was more bluff than substance: Tony much, much preferred the NFL. But if it came down to Seattle or the CFL, you never know, he might have gone north for a year or two. If he had, Seattle would have blown a crucial draft choice, a disastrous fiasco for a fledgling team.

No one knew this better than the Seahawks. And the week before the draft, they began to buckle; they started talking trade with several teams. It might have been the threat of Canada, or maybe they just didn't want a rookie who didn't want them. On the morning of the draft, Seattle decided Dallas had the most to offer. It was a four-for-one deal: Seattle gave up its number two pick in round one for the Cowboys' spot deeper in round one, and three more picks in round two. That afternoon, the Cowboys selected Tony.

Rosenbloom, meanwhile, was now interested in my up-coming negotiations with Dallas. A lot of football people were. The day after the 1977 draft, I'd made the Ricky Bell deal with Tampa: five years, $1.2 million, the richest rookie contract in NFL history. GMs around the league were astounded; Jim Finks of the Bears called the figures "alarming." But even as the other GMs were ridiculing Tampa Bay, I made it public that I expected a similar deal for Dorsett. Insiders were skeptical: the Cowboys were known for, and proud of, their rigid salary structure.

In his office, Rosenbloom turned out to be one of the doubters. "My boy," he said, "you're never going to get the kind of money for Dorsett that you got for Bell. Hell, those people down in Dallas won't pay you half of what you got for Bell."

"I won't get *half*?" I repeated. "Mr. Rosenbloom, you know that's not true. You know I won't settle for anything close to that."

"All right, maybe you'll get half," he said. "But on a five-year contract, no matter how it's cut up, there's no way you'll get a million for Dorsett. In fact, let's make a little bet on it. I'll bet you $500 you don't get a million. Do we have a bet?''

"Mr. Rosenbloom, you're on."

I won: I wound up getting $1.1 million for Tony over five years. I xeroxed a copy of the contract and took it to Rosenbloom's office. I was told he was on vacation. I saw Klosterman, told him about the bet, and said I was there to collect my money. Klosterman eyed the contract and smiled. He picked up the phone and called Rosenbloom.

"Yeah, CR, I've got it right here," Klosterman said. "Yes, it adds up to over a million. Sure thing. Mike, CR wants to talk to you."

"Hello, Mr. Rosenbloom."

All I heard was hard, genuine laughter. When Rosenbloom finally spoke, he sounded like a kid who just got bike for Christmas.

"Well, well, well, my boy, so you earned yourself an extra $500. I'm happy for you, Mike. You got a good contract."

I thanked him.

"Now let me explain something," he went on.

The amusement vanished from Rosenbloom's tone. "That's the best $500 I've ever spent in my life. I *wanted* you to fuck those sons of bitches down in Dallas. Those bastards don't even belong in the league. They're a bunch of self-righteous, hypocritical sons-of-bitches. I wanted to lose that bet, my boy. I wanted to lose it big."

Personally, I had found Gil Brandt, the Cowboys' contract man, to be a hell of a good guy. Rosenbloom wasn't so enamored, of Brandt or anyone else there. In vivid, four-letter detail, he proceeded to shred the Cowboys' entire front office. He said he could hardly wait until the next league meetings; then he could tell the Dallas people, who always bragged about holding the bottom line, that they were a bunch of assholes.

You walk into Donald Trump's office and say, "Hey asshole, I'm a big-time sports agent; you need me, and you need my player—this is what you have to pay." If he's slightly amused, Trump's only going to laugh in your face. More likely, he's going to throw you out of his office.

18
SORRY, FELLAS

I said before that I didn't let management push me around. I also, except for isolated incidents, didn't really try to bully management.

I have a healthy ego. But when I walked into the office of management, I would leave it at the door. My operating style was simple: humility. I was just a nice, regular guy, hoping to make the best deal possible for my client.

In that respect, I was also separate from a majority of agents. You'd be amazed at how many agents storm in like madmen, screaming and insulting, trying to make people look inferior. I didn't try to challenge management's ego, I catered to it. I did that for the sake of my clients. Once you threaten management's ego, it's not just business, it's personal.

It's a fight the agent is almost always going to lose. You're an agent. You walk into Donald Trump's office and say, "Hey asshole, I'm a big-time sports agent; you need me, and you need my player—this is what you have to pay." If he's slightly amused, Trump's only going to laugh in your face.

217

More likely, he's going to throw you out of his office.

I saw it all the time: agents would swagger in, ask for something outrageous, like $1 million for three years, and wind up caving in for $150,000. Because they wasted people's valuable time, then caved in anyway, they had no credibility and therefore no respect. I had a credo: I like to *make* deals, not break them. I won't waste your time with foolish demands, but my initial offer is close to what I want. We can drag this out, but how much is your aggravation worth? Let's not screw around. Add the difference in right now, and I'll get out of your hair. You can go back to running your business.

It was instrumental to my success. And I'm not talking about the periods during which a pair of leagues were competing, when anyone short of a monkey could get a good contract. I mean the times when there was no real leverage, when an agent depended only on his savvy. I made some deals with the Cowboys in which I got a lot more money out of Gil Brandt than other agents had, and yet he still had nice things to say about me afterward. The same went for John Mecom of the Saints after I negotiated Chuck Muncie's deal, which at the time was considered an outrageous contract. Those were the most satisfying moments: when you, your client, and management could all sit down and have a glass of champagne. Everyone felt they had made a decent deal; everyone had acted like gentlemen.

Unfortunately, it wasn't always like that. *I* wasn't always like that. Sometimes things moved too fast, got strange, went spinning out of control. There were times when I behaved like anything *but* a gentleman.

In a business as rough as sports, you do things you later regret. I was a 21-year-old kid who shot right to the top: people wrote about how good I was, and I believed them. Even then, I could see through my own bullshit and knew I was making mistakes. But I never apologized for them. I felt I couldn't. Management was my adversary. I couldn't concede it that edge.

Now, while I've got this opportunity, I'd like to offer

some apologies. They should have come a long time ago.

In 1977, the New York Jets made Wesley Walker, my client, their second-round pick. After Wesley made All-Rookie, he sent me back to Steve Gutman, the Jets' GM, to try to renegotiate. Gutman said, no, his hands were tied: the Jets' Board of Directors had a firm policy against renegotiations. I pressed him, but Gutman said he couldn't buck team policy.

I told Wesley what Gutman had said, and the next thing I knew, Wesley had hired an attorney, who wrote the Jets a letter asking to renegotiate. And the Jets turned around and gave Wesley a new contract.

I wasn't just outraged; I was terribly embarrassed. The Jets had not only lied to me; they'd made me look like a jackass. It's not like they had renegotiated Wesley's contract two years later. This was two weeks. And not with a Slusher or even a Steinberg, but some unknown who'd never done a contract in his life. I vowed that if I ever had another rookie drafted by the Jets, I would make them pay.

In 1980 I got my chance. The Jets made my client, Johnny Lam Jones, their first-round pick. Gutman came to Los Angeles to talk. I outlined a deal: $1.5 million over six years. It was high for the times, and I knew it. I also insisted on it. Punishment money, in a little different form.

"Can I tell you something?" Gutman asked.

"What?"

"You're crazy," he said. "There's no way we can pay this kind of money."

"Fine," I said. "Good-bye. Go home."

Gutman stayed, and eventually the Jets gave me what I wanted: $1.5 million over six years. But not before I humiliated Gutman. In the course of our meeting, I started screaming at him, in vile, offensive language. I was out of control. I acted like an animal.

Steve Gutman is a nice guy, who may have made a mistake but wasn't out to screw anyone. Probably, he got caught in the middle between forces in the Jets organization. For my behavior, I owe him an apology.

When Leonard Tose still owned the Philadelphia Eagles, a woman named Susan Fletcher ran the team for him. Before the 1984 season, Fletcher sent a letter to Mike Quick, my client. In part, it said: "In the event you make the Pro Bowl at the end of next year, come back and we'll renegotiate your contract."

Quick made the Pro Bowl, but when we went to the Eagles to renegotiate, Tose had sold the team to Norman Braman. Fletcher was out. I told Braman about Fletcher's promise, thinking he'd honor it to keep a quality player happy. Braman gave me a screw-you smile and told me to go see Susan Fletcher. He said he owned the Eagles now, and he wasn't going to renegotiate.

Quick didn't report to the Eagles' training camp. At the beginning of August, I got a call from Harry Gamble, the Eagles' GM. He urged me to fly immediately to Philadelphia. Braman, he said, was ready to talk.

I told Gamble I didn't want to make the trip unless we had a substantial possibility for progress. I was going to South Africa later that week to work on a documentary. I didn't want to fly to Philadelphia, back to LA, back to New York a day later, and then to South Africa. More important, if I flew to Philadelphia, I would miss my daughter's birthday. Gamble assured me that Braman was serious.

Sure he was. I flew all the way to Philadelphia to hear Braman say he'd love to redo Mike's contract, but not at that time. After next season, perhaps. If he had told me that on the telephone, fine. As it was, I went completely berserk. First I started cursing him, then I nearly overturned his desk.

I'm still sorry I missed my daughter's birthday for no good reason. But that doesn't justify my outburst in Braman's office. I've never been more childish, uncivil, or boorish in my entire career. Norman Braman, I apologize.

Ladd Herzeg is the general manager of the Houston Oilers. From our business relationship grew a fairly good friendship. That is, until Herzeg heard about Carroll Rosenbloom's scheme to steal Earl Campbell from the Oilers. And that Rosenbloom had proposed the plot to me, a guy whom Herzeg had thought of as a friend.

I didn't know Rosenbloom was going to make that kind of offer before I went to his home. Once it was made, I had to weigh the interests of my client, which meant keeping Rosenbloom's plan to myself, regardless of my friendship with Herzeg. I opted for secrecy and also used Rosenbloom's interest to get Earl a superior contract. In retrospect, I think I made the wrong decision. I should have called Herzeg and told him exactly what had transpired. After he read about my meeting with Rosenbloom, my relationship with Herzeg deteriorated rapidly. I take the blame for that. And for breaching our friendship, I apologize.

I had another regretful episode with Houston. There were some documents to be drawn up in addition to Earl's standard contract. The deal was verbally consummated, even written out in longhand; it just needed to be typed. Herzeg's assistant GM, Pat Peppler, was to supervise the secretary as she typed them, while Earl, Herzeg, and I went out to lunch.

When we returned from the restaurant, I looked at the documents. It seemed to me that Peppler had pulled a fast one: he'd edited and condensed some of the provisions and, in the process, reneged on what we'd just agreed to. When Herzeg pleaded ignorance, I exploded at Peppler. I berated him, loudly and cruelly, in front of the people he worked with. Peppler, many years older than I, was ready to leave the building and fight.

We wound up getting our original contract, but I didn't feel the usual sense of accomplishment. I was ashamed of myself. Peppler, who'd coached under Vince Lombardi, had put his entire life into the game of football. It must have been terribly humiliating to have some young, arrogant son-of-a-bitch like me denigrate him in front of his peers. Eventually we became good friends, but I wouldn't have blamed Pat if he had never spoken to me again. He's a good man. He deserves an apology.

Al Ward, the Jets' GM before Gutman, also deserved better than what I gave him. Ward tried twice to sign Anthony Davis. Both times he failed, when Davis went to the Southern California Suns, and later to the Toronto Argonauts. The first time, the Jets weren't even close to our price. The second time, Ward made a legitimate attempt to sign Davis, but his superiors cut off his budget. Ward really wanted Davis; he just didn't have the power.

It was early in Ward's career with the Jets; losing Davis twice couldn't have made him look good. I've always felt bad about two things: that we couldn't cut a deal, and the way I treated Ward in our second negotiation. I knew I had a lever, the Argonauts, and I was rude and unyielding because of it. Al Ward, I'm sorry.

I detailed earlier my quarrel with Don Klosterman, when he accused me of revealing Johnnie Johnson's contract. In retrospect, I wish the whole thing had never happened. Klosterman, perhaps more than anybody I've ever dealt with in management, truly seemed to care about his players' best interest. If I could do it all again, I wouldn't say a single word to the reporter from the *Los Angeles Times*. Klosterman, a very decent man, had gone out on a limb and given Johnnie an unprecedented contract. Simply out of my respect for Klosterman, I should have handled things differently. And for some of the things that I said in the aftermath, I apologize.

I still consider Mike Brown less than a reasonable man in terms of negotiating salaries. But in my dealings with him, there is one thing I'm sorry about. It was in the heat of the Anthony Munoz affair, when emotions were running high. As I said, during the Munoz incident, Brown was leaking stories to the press. One article appeared with the headline: "Let the Big Burrito Stay in LA." They were referring to Munoz, insinuating that I was screwing him. Someone—

Brown, I'm sure—sent it to Munoz with no return address.

I lost my temper. When I was called by the Cincinnati press for a comment, I said Brown was the dog of NFL managers, and a flea-bitten dog to boot. Coming from a highly visible agent, it was major news the following day in Cincinnati. In fact, I heard later that whenever Brown would enter the locker room for the next few weeks, several of the Bengals would wait until he wasn't looking, then pretend they were dogs, flicking off fleas.

Brown is a street fighter who grabs at every advantage; at the time, I felt an apology might give him an edge in our future encounters. I'm apologizing now, because Brown should not have had to read that type of thing in the town where he lives. Brown was fighting in the streets, and I stooped a little lower, into the gutter. I was out of line; to Mike Brown, I apologize.

Time. Now that I'm not an active agent, what the hell will I do with mine?

I'll think things through this time, see where I want to go. Agenting just happened, on a fluke; I never sat down and planned what to do with my life. Frankly, I never thought I'd stay at it as long as I did. During the first five years, the business was fun. I was a kid, early 20s, winning, proving my point, in an older man's game. And I was representing professional athletes, the same type of people I'd idolized when I was a child.

As I got older, I began to see things as they were, not only as I wanted them to be. I saw a finite number of players go pro each year, yet an infinite number of people trying to earn a living off those players. To make a buck, I saw what that competition could do to human nature. It stole the fun away. I seemed too young to be jaded.

I got tired, tired of a business that often resembled a cesspool. Tired of the self-righteous hypocrites. Tired of defending my name against fraudulent charges. Tired of getting attacked for admitting to the same damn things everyone else was doing but didn't have the honesty to own up to. When I look back at those people, the Leigh Steinbergs, the Steve Feldmans, the Jack Millses, the Tom Osbornes, irrespective of what they've said about me, I know in my heart I never prostituted myself to their level, never cast false aspersions about another man in order to make a dollar.

Though I view the business with mixed emotions, I don't regret my career. There were too many good things. I made my mark, provided for my family, met some fine people, had some laughs. Out of a job, I suppose that's about all you can ask for.

But that chapter is over now. My life right now is what's important. Maybe I'll try my hand at Hollywood, producing films. Hell, maybe we can make a movie out of this book.

I wonder if Eddie Murphy has ever played a sports agent.